COLLECTING
Dirt

COLLECTING
Dirt

Kuiper Mihai

iUniverse, Inc.
Bloomington

Collecting Dirt

iUniverse books may be ordered through booksellers or by contacting:

iUniverse
1663 Liberty Drive
Bloomington, IN 47403
www.iuniverse.com
1-800-Authors (1-800-288-4677)

ISBN: 978-1-4620-2746-0 (pbk)
ISBN: 978-1-4620-2747-7 (ebk)

Printed in the United States of America

iUniverse rev. date: 06/17/2011

Chapter One

The smell of old, rustic wood combined with newly installed carpet makes it quite simple for me to guess where I am. I look around the rows of families to see some members catching a quick snooze while others listen intently to an echoing voice, trying to grasp every word spoken, as if a misinterpreted vowel decided the difference of one going to heaven or going to hell. My fingers begin to tap upon my best pair of jeans, which are matched with a collared, short-sleeved shirt—nothing any ordinary ten year old should be wearing on one of only two days of rest between the routine of school. I'm surprised to see my patience has lasted these entire 4 minutes of being here; I just might set a new record.

In the row just ahead of the one I am sitting in, I see a boy, about my age, playing on a Gameboy. His tongue sticks out every now and then, and his body sometimes leans to one side, the tell-tale sign that he almost placed the 'z' shaped widget in the wrong slot, making it more of a hassle to get rid of that line of blocks. That extra nudge of his body ensures the proper resting place for each block. I can tell he succeeded because he didn't give out that usual pout and smack of the lips when boys don't get what they want. He, too, is wearing a nice get-up, and has his hair parted to the right side, reminding me of some movies I saw in the 1980's. This boy's actions are not unique; I have seen this time and time again, whether it is blatant like this boy, or masked behind baggy long sleeves by others to avoid confrontation from unhappy parents.

Two rows ahead of the gamer, I see another young boy, maybe a year or two younger than I am. This boy looks as if he doesn't want anything to do with what is being said from the podium, either, and his actions surely have already brought attention to him. He is writhing around in his chair the way a retarded dancer in the night would do, free from all judgmental eyes. The boy has his arms and back arched as if he is trying to touch the back of his heels. This gesture reminds me of how infants squirm in their parents' arms once they had enough loving and were ready to be set free from the overwhelming grasp. What disturbs me is how the boy's mother sits as if nothing is going on. She sits like a studious monk ignoring the flails of a mad child. That kid needs to be dragged out of this place and smacked around with the rings of four fingers. He needs to be stripped of all his dignity to show him that the world isn't his own personal rubix cube. Am I going to hell for having these thoughts in such a sanctuary? Nah, I'll be alright . . .

I look up to the robed, old man standing behind the podium to take my mind off leaping over these few rows of zombies like a flying squirrel and putting that menace of a child in a choke hold that won't ever quit. The man up front is called 'Father', but I have never understood why. I can come up with my own reason, but I can guarantee it's neither the right nor appropriate reason. His robed ensemble seems to have layers, kind of reminding me of my mother's out-dated drapes she has hanging from the windows of our house, with black sheets as his nighty and a gradual transformation into a bold purple on the outer-most layer. He mostly reads from his book, though sometimes musters up the courage to add his own words to his lecture. His sentences are slow and drawn out with a high intonation throughout, except for the sudden drop right before each sentence break. It is as if he is asking the audience a question, but half way through the sentence he remembers that he is supposed to be *telling* us what to do, rather than asking. Every now and then he sneaks a quick peek to one of his sides, having a glance at one of his two 12 year old assistants. I know he does this to reset his confidence once it begins to slip as he notices his onlookers in the bleachers getting restless.

He is not a powerful looking man, standing only about five feet, four inches tall and wearing primitive eyeglasses. Head lice would have prime real estate in his cul de sac hair. And he definitely has passed the half-century mark in age. So how can this wee old man have total control over these robots? What kind of mind games is this man playing? Did he slip some sort of potion into those chips that he feeds to his pets every week? Whatever the trick is, I am not falling for it.

The beautiful smell of water lilies enters my nostrils. I have a look around and see that it must be coming from the pretty young girl sitting four seats to the right of me. She must have just hopped out of a morning shower 20 minutes ago. There is no slouch in her back as she sits. She looks like the student who constantly has my teacher's attention at school, with her hands clasped and nestling gently upon her lap. Her sleek blonde hair parts at the center of her unblemished forehead, making sure no strands distract her view. Her blue eyes are focused and gathering all information from the speaker up front. A half-smile is constant as she is hypnotized by each word the Father speaks. Anyone who has the capability of being hypnotized can easily fall into the trance simply by listening to a voice which lacks fluctuating tones, much like our preacher's.

These past few minutes have reinforced something that has been swarming around in my mind for a while now. I have realized that I am not like most children in this vast room. I don't waste away my time with empty satisfaction that leads to nowhere like the boy playing the hand-held device. I don't bamboozle around like a circus animal trying to win a treat like the silly boy seeking attention. And I surely don't believe something that a person tells me without questioning it or voicing my own opinions and rebuttals first.

Although I am at a young age, I have already realized that I am quite different from most of the school children I see loitering around the halls of my junior high. I overhear groups of boys talking about some sort of fantasy card game and what newly-added abilities a particular class of elf now possesses and I think to myself, come on, you dorks. Go out and get a life.

I overhear groups of girls laughing and giggling about gossip they had just heard and I think to myself just how ridiculous it is to keep tabs and news updates about people who rarely or never interact with you.

I overhear groups of boys talking about a test they recently took and how well they thought they did on it. School is something that shouldn't be stressed about. Any quizzes or exams given to students should not be taken so serious to the point when a young adult contemplates suicide for fear of family failure, like in some eastern countries. All tested material is discussed in class and when the test does arrive, you either retained the information or you didn't. It's quite simple, I think.

And here I am sitting, with this mass gathering of people, listening to folklore and tales. I don't understand how all these people—and not just *these* people, but millions around the world—fall prey to the teachings and customs of this silliness. Those who are currently attending do this sort of thing every week. They must wake up early on a day free from their stressful jobs and schools to dress fancily for who knows who and to sit amongst others for a listen about ancient stories that are supposed to help us live a 'better' life. I am only here because my parents think this will 'make me become a good adult'. But look at all these people actually playing along. These are grown adults with supposed intellectual minds who are doing this. I would understand if this room was filled with three year olds who didn't know what the fuck was going on. But this is quite the opposite. I think I'm going to be sick.

Chapter Two - Many Years Later

My name is Frank Stiles. I am currently 29 years old. I live in southern California and I hold a great career. I stand at a little over six feet tall and in the past 10 years, my weight has never stabilized, always ranging from about 175 to about 210 pounds. Lately, I have been tipping the scale towards the latter, but it's probably because I've started to settle down with this new career thing. My build is a bit average, I must admit, but there's not much I can do to fend off the ladies when they have a look at my stunning good looks. I am not trying to be narcissistic or anything, but even I can't help but smile every time I look into a mirror. Okay, maybe that is a textbook definition of the word . . .

I recently got a job with the Los Angeles Sheriff's Department. This has allowed me to relax and have a stable income. The work is posh at the moment, only expecting me to stand on guard duty at a local hospital in the greater Los Angeles area. I try to make my own fun amidst the boredom by venturing up to the floor of the building which has numerous stories of paranormal activity happening. Deputies tell me they would be in the empty gym upstairs and hear the clanking sounds of barbells hitting one another. Random doors opening and closing, bursts of cold air, and lights flickering—the most commonly heard and seen events—are all occurring in my workspace.

Boasting this pristine cop's uniform as I go to and from work, I feel as if I am on top of the world and have unimaginable power over all other law abiding citizens. As others look at me while I'm wearing my combat suit, I always wonder what goes through their mind, if anything. Are they thinking I'm one of those cops who will drop everything to recover a purse that had been snatched by a typical low life who desperately needs to pay off his child support bills? Are they thinking I carry this badge to get into places no one else can get to, then later conjuring up an elaborate maze of a story with countless interlinking mini series' to get on top with a massive cache of stolen loot like some sort of Denzel Washington drama? Or maybe they are thinking that I am the perfect police officer who lives a perfect life free of crime and only means to do well amongst his community. Well, that last one is definitely not true for me, but I have met others who live that lifestyle.

I have lived my life to the fullest, for almost three decades now. I have been free as a bird ever since my childhood, to think and to do whatever I liked. I didn't have any rules or fears of damnation. I wasn't constrained, mentally nor physically. Don't get me wrong, though, I am not a bad person. I don't get off doing horrid things to others. I know right from wrong, through first hand experiences. Have I ever stolen? Of course I have. Do I know it is wrong? Of course I do. That churning feeling I had in my stomach that time I stole a special edition Superman comic told me that I shouldn't do it again. Do I know it is wrong to inflict pain unto others? Absolutely. That arthritic pain and swelling in my hand I had that morning after I punched some guy in the face at a nearby bar not too long ago told me to not do that often. Well, that one wasn't a good example. But surely that oozy feeling I had the night of—and not from just the beer—was the sign. It is this freedom that has allowed me to see all the weird things and tell all my weird stories that make everyone laugh and shake their heads.

I have to be honest: I don't think I really should be a sheriff. No, no, it's not what you think. Not because I'll use my 'power for evil' (insert that mischievous laugh). It is because I never should have gotten the job in the first place, given my past.

Walking into the first day of basic sheriff training you will see people from all backgrounds. When it was my first day of training, there were clean cut rookies ready to impress, obvious drug addicts that needed to fund their habit, and even head-shaven gangsters with Norteno tattooed across their chest. But those who actually get the job and carry onward to the second day as a county sheriff have lived pretty pristine lives, for the most part. They usually don't have a record of any crime or malpractice. They are generally inexperienced people right out of college or the military. I say inexperienced because the majority of them haven't seen or know about the things they might encounter while serving their community.

I remember during basic training of becoming a sheriff there was a guest speaker in one of our daily classes to tell us about some of the drugs we may encounter during our patrols. Of course, this speaker worked with the sheriff's drug unit, so I guess one can go on a limb and say he was an 'expert' on the topic. He was discussing one of the more common drugs we would find on the streets: marijuana. I will skip to the part of the lecture that is of importance to the story, which came in at about midway through the speech.

Our guest displayed two pictures of marijuana plants, cannabis. He pointed to the picture on the left and said, "This is a photo of what a male cannabis plant looks like."

He then pointed to the picture of the right. "This is a photo of what a female cannabis plant looks like," he continued. "As you can see, they are nearly indistinguishable."

After a long pause, a student asked, "Is there any way one can tell the difference between a male and female plant?"

The speaker responded, "I do not have that information for you at this time."

I was thinking, this asshole is supposed to be an expert in his field of narcotics and he can't tell the difference between a dude plant and a chick plant? Wow, you have got to be kidding me.

I looked around the room of blank stares and could tell I was the only one in the room that knew the female cannabis plant boasts white hairs all throughout the pistils they grow. These hairs are used to catch the seeds the males give off to fertilize the female and begin the reproduction process.

This information was revealed to me during a smoking session I had with a good high school friend. How he knew is a mystery to me.

Did I enlighten my so-called teacher? Hell no. I wasn't ready to blow my cover so soon in training.

So again, don't judge me for calling these newbies inexperienced—or newbies—for that matter. They will probably learn about this information eventually, but in a boring way.

Although I *did* manage to become a deputy sheriff, it wasn't easy. In the beginning of my search, I had applied for the San Bernardino County Sheriff's Department, which is the largest county in the continental United States by area. San Bernardino County borders Los Angeles, to the east. It was my first choice because it would have been closer to where I reside.

After I began the application and paperwork process, all the appropriate tests were then commenced: background checks, physical tests and psychological evaluations. I never made it to the latter ones; the processing came to a halt as the department had a look at my past records. At the moment I am not at liberty to announce exactly what is on this notorious file, but it will soon unravel itself as we move along. It was an upset, but I knew I would never get past the initial tests all along without a bit of help.

I never understood why employers—especially government employers—look and scrutinize so deeply into all the paperwork that piles up as we go through our lives. All of the illegal things in the past should not disqualify me from being a part of the law enforcement team. It should make me even *more* qualified because I can more easily relate to criminals out on the streets. I know what is going through their minds during that drug deal. I know when and where they will destroy private property to send a message to an opposing faction. I know where and just how fast they are able to drive when trying to outrun a pursuing vehicle. All of this is relevant knowledge and experience. It can all be used in the line of duty.

The San Bernardino County Sheriff's Department should not have based their decision on the negatives in my past. They definitely lost out on a well-qualified individual. I did four years of service in the Army Infantry, enduring some of the greatest hardships any person could go through. I have sculpted and perfected combat skills during those years which were easily transferred from the military life to the civilian police life.

Ever since my childhood years, I wanted to become a police officer and I set my mind to do so ever since. Not only the years of physical and mental training, but my natural combat skills made me a prime candidate for law enforcement. I realized this ability after having a few sparring matches with some of the best in the field.

Growing up, I always enjoyed watching the cheesy late 80's, early 90's, Van Damme and Seagal fighting flicks shown at prime time. I would mimic the fancy moves each would portray against their rivals in my head, visualizing myself flying through the air, twisting my body around until the heel of my foot cracked the jaw of my opponent. I never took martial arts or fighting serious enough to take formal classes, but when I reached high school, my friends and I wrestled a couple times, just to see what it was like. It was all fun and games, but I found it rather easy to put my friends into a choke hold and tap them out. It only took a couple of matches to realize that I was pretty good at that sort of thing.

One day I happened to come across my high school's wrestling state champion. I would guess this guy knew what he was doing when fighting, our school being one of the best in the nation. He had an average wrestler's build, being only about five foot, six inches, but having lots of muscle mass all around him. He must have weighed just a bit more than I, even with me towering about five inches above him. We were talking about fighting and wrestling one day, then out of nowhere, I told him, "Man, I bet you I can tap you out if we wrestled."

He gave a quick laugh which led to a face of complete disbelief. "Okay. After school, come to my place and we'll see what happens," he agreed to the challenge.

Later that day, we met at his house and headed straight for his backyard. There were no angry emotions at all; this was just going to be a quick, fun check to see who would come out on top. Friends from both sides were also there to witness what was about to go down. We took off any excess clothing to get comfortable and then took our corners.

I rang an imaginary bell to commence the match and he immediately started by putting me in a head lock and tried to throw me to the ground. I did my best to resist from being taken to the floor, the worst spot to be during a fight. We grappled for a few seconds, each of us trying to bring the other down to the ground. Then, in a blink of an eye, I swung myself around him, still holding on to his arms and put him in a lock. I knew there was no way of escaping the hold I had on him. The tap came shortly after, when I applied downward pressure to his arms, which were twisted behind him by that time.

"Wow, man, not bad," he said to me.

"Yeah, man, good job. I told you that you wouldn't beat me," I said back to him, smiling and out of breath.

After that, the word got around our school that I had tapped out the state champion. One of his friends soon came up to me and wanted to try to take me on. This guy was huge. He must have been about six feet tall and weighed well over two hundred pounds. He would intimidate any normal person.

"I bet you can't make me tap out," he told me.

"I don't know but I'll try. I bet you I can," I said back, in my usual cocky manner.

So, again, I had a wrestling match set up to see if I can take out another trained fighter. The usual crowds of friends were all around us, cheering and anxious to see the results. We geared down and got ready. The match began and he started tossing me around like a chew toy. He easily overpowered me. The scene must have looked funny to all the spectators because surely it looked as if he was just playing around with me. I was literally being thrown around from side to side. He would put me in a quick grapple, and then launch me to the side. This happened for quite some time. I knew I needed to find a way to get him to the ground. I knew that once I had him on the ground, I would be able to put him into a lock that would be inescapable.

He threw another headlock my way, and I used that opportunity to swoop his legs out from under him with one of mine. As soon as he hit the floor, I knew I had him. Not two seconds later, I had both of my legs wrapped around him like a pretzel, squeezing like a snake. The hand tap was inevitable. I proved myself.

Periodic feats of natural combat strength happened after that, including the time I was doing combat training in the military with my brown belt Jiu-Jitsu instructor. I actually sparred with him one day because our group of soldiers was oddly matched. With the different types of maneuvers and grapples I was able to place on my instructor, he had thought I had years of experience after putting him in an unprecedented choke hold that left him shocked and breathless. But we don't need to get into detail of that at this time.

Nevertheless, I did manage to nab a job as a Deputy Sheriff for Los Angeles County, despite the bad news from the neighboring county. The process through Los Angeles County was much easier than I expected. I admirably thank an insider for this. I have a close tie to a well-respected sergeant for the same county, and he not only guided me through the hiring process, but he also did his best to set up particular points in the hiring with conditions that would benefit me. But even with a great hook up from the inside, there were still some dead ends that were almost unavoidable. There were times when I had almost given up, times when I thought my past would finally come back to bite me in the ass.

Chapter Three

I would neither consider myself being good nor bad as a child. Well, I guess you can say that I had a little of both in me. There was a part of me that did well at school—as far as grades were concerned. This same part had and still has great morals, beliefs and practices.

I was very active in sports as a child and participated in baseball, track, and went pretty far as a soccer player. These sorts of things were all fun and games any child or young adult would love to do, and I fully stayed interested in these sports until the fun was no longer present. Obviously the games themselves didn't lose the fun factor, but it was when special trainers and coaches showed up and treated these hobbies as something more, something much more serious than what they actually were—at least for me. Once this had occurred, my sports career came to a halt.

General misbehavior balanced the good and the bad. There were silly things I would do with my friends that might seem common to any other teenage boy wanting to cause a bit of trouble. My past actions may seem unique in their own way, but every neighborhood troublemaker has their own similar variance to pass the time between school days.

Living of a hill—in a city of hills, actually—made mischief a bit easier to get away with, using the extremities of hill crests as quick hideaways. Like in the case when some friends and I made a cardboard cutout copy of an animal to scare the neighbors. Our favorite gimmick was a house cat. This cutout would be fairly accurate, giving the correct proportions to limbs and body structure. The niche we had with our mock cat was the foil we placed where eyes would be so they could reflect any light shone on them.

Once our project fit our likings, we took to the hills, usually at night. We would go to one hill in particular, a paved one where lots of cars traveled. We would stand the cat up in the middle of the lane where cars travel. The cat would stand just after the crest of the hill, so oncoming drivers had very little time to react to the cat they were about to hit. This was all good fun, especially when we got cars to skid out of control, almost crashing into the curb and hopping onto the sidewalk.

Whenever I decided to take out any angst on cars some more, there was another trick I would use (by this point it may seem as if cars were my enemy). This is a quick jab to do if you're bored. I used to take a bit of duct tape and roll about two or three feet's worth unto itself, creating a double sided strip. I would get a couple of these, maybe three or four. The tape would then be stuck on a road, preferably a road where drivers don't travel very fast and the neighborhood is quiet. I would then line up these pieces, trying to stick them where I thought a car's tires would roll over. Once they were stuck in place, I ran aside and took a front row seat. What would happen was the cars would roll over the tape and make a loud popping noise. I found the popping noise to almost exactly resemble a tire that had just blown. Drivers would be startled and have the tendency to jerk the steering wheel to one side, almost crashing into the curb, just like my previous example.

This was the extent of my mischief. I did lots of things to this nature. I mean, I never killed anyone, raped anyone or even joined a gang. Just simple things that my mother would not approve of were what I stuck to.

There was an instance that almost went too far, though. I remember a time when I was a few years older from the time of playing with cars. This might have been the first or second year of high school. I was out at a party with a few of my best friends at the time. We'll call them Rodney, Patrick, Ham, Grainy and Peter for now. We were all relaxing, having a few beers and talking with one another.

Out of nowhere, Peter tells Ham, "Yo, man. Go up to that guy over there and clock him in the head. If any of his friends jump in, we've got your back."

This might sound a bit odd to a normal person, yes, but this was the kind of I-don't-care attitude my friends and I had. What made Peter tell this to Ham? Who knows . . . Who cares, really . . . Well, I guess maybe the guy who was about to get his face smashed.

Sure enough, Ham walked straight up to this guy who was simply minding his own business. We didn't even know this bloke's name. We may have seen him up and down the hallways of school before, but never even interacted with him—until now, of course.

Ham isn't the biggest of my friends, but he can definitely pull his own weight when the time demanded so. He was about five feet five inches at the time, but he was very built from lifting weights at his gym a few nights a week. The clothes he wore were rather large, but he didn't have a difficult time filling most of them in. He would look intimidating to anyone, surely, if they saw him fast approaching. Just imagine someone in the Mexican Mafia and how they look, with the shaved head, large build, callous eyes and erroneous scars, but minus the tattoos. That picture was pretty much what Ham looked like.

The initial punch from Ham was all Peter had to see to jump in to the beating. The two of them wailed on this poor unsuspecting guy that didn't even have a chance to throw a single punch back. It wasn't too bad, though. Ham and Peter didn't put this dude out of commission for the rest of his life; they did him just enough to cause a total face swelling with a few deep gashes in the upper cheeks and nose. These guys are ruthless, not brutal.

Soon after, we left.

We decided to go back to Grainy's house to relax with some more beers. About a half hour into our chill session, we heard the squeals of countless cars drive up. The high pitched sound of upgraded exhausts filled the night air. The humming came to a low murmur, and then there was banging on the front door.

Grainy walked up and opened the front door. An angry mob of probably 20 Mexicans stood there, baseball bats in hands. One of them spoke up and asked Grainy, "Where's Peter and Ham at?"

Grainy calmly answered back, "They aint in here. And if you try to fuck anything up, my dad's in the Lucky Eights, nigga. He'll hunt you down and kill all you."

While this quick exchange of words was happening, Peter and Ham slipped out through the backyard and ran. Rodney, Patrick and I stayed in the living room, keeping cool, lounging on a massive white sofa with a beer in hand. I perked an ear up, trying to listen to what was about to go down. A few more words thrown back and forth that I couldn't make out, then I heard the uninvited guest yell, "Move outta my way, nigga!"

As soon as we heard those words, the three of us jumped from the sofa, ran out into the backyard, hopped over the fence and started to run. Our relaxed nature was soon countered and replaced with panic.

Running through the bushes that separated different communities, we heard the 2.0 liter engines of Hondas turn over and scream up and down the streets, traveling in what sounded like all directions.

My heart was pounding harder than it ever had before. Adrenaline rushed through my blood veins, allowing me to run and jump as if I were an Olympic star. I was a little scared, but it looked as if I was a hundred times calmer than Rodney. His eyes seemed as if they were about to pop out of their sockets trying to catch as much information and ways out as possible. It was a cool, brisk night, like any other in Southern California, but that didn't stop the steady streams of sweat from carving paths down Rodney's face. His entire body was fidgety, especially his hands and fingers. At certain moments, his hands would contort like a child with a mental problem. Rodney would bombard me and Patrick with questions, trying to find reassurance and comfort.

"Dude, where do we go?! What do we do now?! Do you think they'll find us?! What if they find us? What do you think they'll do?! Should we go that way?!" Rodney fired at us.

We stopped at random houses, knocking on the doors, trying to find a way to use a phone to get a ride the hell out of there. Numerous houses we stopped at had their lights on inside, but no one would answer the door once we knocked. The blaring of music and screeching of wheels throughout the streets was probably what kept dwellers indoors. Those bastards. Every second we wasted waiting for a life line was a chance for one of the imported cars to drive by and spot us.

At this moment, I thought about Ham and Peter, hoping that they had already found a way out of this mess. Yeah, true, it is them who started all this nonsense. But, still, they had all my best wishes. My close group of friends always stuck together and would do anything for one other, no matter what the cost. These values still hold to this day and always will.

We finally reached a giving hand that led us to a phone and safety for a few minutes while our ride was on the way. The old lady that let us into her home offered some water and comfortable chairs to sit in while we waited. She was clearly a grandmother, with pictures of her children and grandchildren strewn about the downstairs, which probably explained her kind demeanor. The smell of old wood, maybe from the antique furniture, lingered in the air. It was actually rather soothing, which was what Rodney desperately needed at the time to calm his nerves.

Our ride snuck through the streets inconspicuously. Soon enough, we quickly all jammed into my friend Larry's extended cab Tacoma truck. The ride home had us acting like jack-in-the-boxes with us bobbing up and down as we saw small caravans of hatchbacks and racers fly by. The buzz and excitement was winding down as we pulled into Ham's driveway, with him and Peter running towards us from the top of our street.

They were exhausted and panting hard. Though tired, they still had a huge smile on their faces, cracking up laughing while they were reciting the maneuvers it took to evade their once impending doom.

"Dude, you should have seen me Superman over this tall-ass barb wire fence!" Peter showed off his accomplishment.

"It will never beat the way I flew up this one tree to hide from one of cars as it sped by me!" Ham countered.

These kinds of things always had us laughing, even if we had almost died. It was the shear rush and the general thought of something new happening which we loved. This is why troublemakers are expected to constantly do deeds of the like. They feel addicted to the adrenaline rush and excitement of the acts. They are addicted to the feeling; just like a smoker is addicted to the soothing sensation of the nicotine entering the blood stream and an alcoholic is addicted to the feeling of lost inhibitions and free spirit they gain from drinking.

While all of these pranks were going on, I was still managing great grades in school, in some rather difficult honors and advanced placement courses. I always found school somewhat easy. I didn't understand how people would do poorly in classes. The material that was to be graded was presented by the teachers and the students knew exactly what was to be on the tests. It was just a matter of allowing the information to seep in and to retain it, which is what I find rather easy. All one has to do is replay whatever is said in class like a tape recorder would, and there you have it: all the information. Sounds simple, right?

These great grades were steadfast throughout most of my high school days. It wasn't until the latter years where they took a steep nose dive into the other end of the spectrum. The introduction of marijuana—weed—was the blame for this. I began to smoke weed about midway through my junior year of high school. And I smoked a lot, all the time. It was a rare occurrence that I would be sober at school. It was a rare occurrence that I would even attend all of my classes. I remember having over 50 annotated absences in my first period class. My motivation for school quickly dwindled. I no longer cared, really. All I really cared about was relaxing and having fun. And that's exactly what I did for the next year.

As my school career was ending, I was having thoughts about what I would be doing after this 13 year gig I was about to finish up. I was in Food and Nutrition class one day and was discussing this with Peter and Ham.

"Dude, I wish I could get paid to go around killing people or something," I had jokingly said to Ham. "Not like some lunatic blasting random people in public, nah. But something like an assassin or sniper or something. I would only take out bad people; only people who truly deserved it."

I had it all worked out in my mind. I would be a type of rogue angel, in flesh and blood.

I have always felt this way. This is yet another thing that separates me from most other people. I think it must have been all those war movies I grew up watching. I don't know if there's something wrong with me, but I also enjoyed having a gun in the grips of my hands.

As children—or I should say teenagers, so I don't get any hate mails that need to be forwarded—my father would take my two brothers and I out into the California deserts to do some hunting. Nothing big, we would go for small game like rabbits, birds or if we were lucky, small coyotes. Rabbits were very common, though. We would take a few pistols, a couple of .22 rifles and a shotgun to choose from once we got there. Of course, I would opt to use the shotgun for its lethality and power. But when any of these firearms were equipped, it seemed as if they were an extension of my arms. I definitely had the most kills out of my siblings and father. I am even positive about having more kills than them put together. I always looked forward to the hunts, which usually occurred during the fall or winter time.

So if there was something I could do which would allow me to carry a gun and be in similar situations, then I would throw all my chips into that bet.

I took the assassin idea and dulled it down a bit when I came up with the idea to join the Marine Infantry. It is common knowledge that the Marines see more combat and fighting than any other branch of the military. I thought that I could start out as an Infantryman and work my way to become a part of the Special Forces. Surely they see lots of action. That was the plan, at least.

About two weeks after visiting a local Marine recruiter, I had returned to the offices to receive my results from my MEPS center visit a week earlier. MEPS is where all recruits go to take care of initial tests before being inducted into basic training. It is where blood work, eye tests, hearing tests, x-rays and an overall physical exam takes place. It is also where all the crazies and drug addicts get weeded out so the government doesn't have to waste money on preliminary general issue items for someone who will end up getting kicked out of service anyway.

I got to the recruiter's office only to hear bad news. "Stiles, you had the highest amount of THC in your blood that I have ever seen in all my years of being a recruiter," he told me.

I didn't know how or what to feel. I certainly felt embarrassed, though. But it was kind of silly of me to think the results would come clean. Maybe I was expecting a miracle to happen.

Needless to say, I never made my way back to the Marine recruiter again after that encounter. Instead, I went two months without smoking weed then headed to the nearby Army recruiter to try all over again. I did the MEPS thing for a second time and had all my tests approved that time around.

After the good news, I sat down with an Army recruiter to discuss my future with them. I explained to them exactly what I wanted as my ultimate goal—to be in the Special Forces. A few different plans were laid out in front of me, so I could choose my fate.

It looked as if the Army presented an offer that I couldn't refuse. I worked it out so I would begin as an Infantryman, and then quickly set out to start Ranger training to begin my life in the Special Forces where opportunities to more prestigious outfits would soon fly open thereafter.

I was golden.

Chapter Four

The first days in the Georgian basic training facilities were great. It was a whole lot of processing and issuing. The Army used this time to brand us and make us theirs for the next few years. They stripped us of our civilian names and implanted our social security numbers into our brains as our new identifications. These were used to make all the processing easier and faster. We were given general issue uniforms of all types. We received the normal camouflage and a few different types of dress uniforms; occasion and season are what determined the particular uniform to wear. Eyeglasses were issued to those who needed them, bed sheets, toiletries and anything else you can think of that you would need to survive for four months.

It was cake so far, nothing to be worried about. I thought this was it. I thought this was all they would throw at us. I was slightly mistaken.

Out of nowhere one morning, there must have been a dozen ogres that flew out of a large cattle car, screaming to the point where I could hear their voices begin to rasp. They all charged at a large group of about 100 recruits, flailing their arms like giant squids trying to wrestle a behemoth whale into submission. Our large number obviously didn't faze them, most of us seemingly cowering in fear.

I remember the first thing these monsters tried to do was to separate us into smaller groups. The way they did this made me quickly realize this entire training program was going to be a big brainwashing session. These Drill Sergeants started blurting out every racial slur imaginable to put us into these particular segregations. The whites were rounded up into their patch, along with the blacks, Hispanics, Asians and so forth. I had already known the reason for this before one of the fiends yelled out in a clearer voice, "You are all no longer separated. All of you clowns are now one. In my Army, you are all equal."

He went on to say, "There will be no individuals in my Army. You are all a small part of one giant blob of cluster-fuck."

The molding had begun.

A large fraction of military basic training is to see if a recruit will be mentally capable of handling the hardships and stresses the Army life throws at them, especially in a war-time situation. Many people think that boot camp has a lot of physical activities involved, like doing all sorts of push-ups, sit-ups, obstacle courses, running everywhere, carrying large loads over long distances and doing exercise after exercise until one can hardly move anymore. Well, if you think this, you're right. But the whole reasoning behind this is to see if your mind can hack the Army environment. The way they do this is by making all of these physical activities based upon group success. The Drill Instructors want to see if you are capable of doing this unselfishly, to make sure you all get through the hardship together. After all, that's how any war is. Surely you have heard of the saying "leave no soldier behind".

Basic Training wasn't entirely about the above, though. There was a lot of learning involved. We attended classes to learn about the entire Army system, like the chain of command, the daily life of a soldier, the different MOS's (jobs), and the proper way to go about our day as a military member. And it also seemed like some of the Drill Instructors took some time off just to play around with some of the recruits. After all, we felt like we had to do everything they told us.

There was a time early in Basic Training when I remember getting pulled aside from my platoon, along with two other recruits. Why we were chosen: I couldn't tell you. Maybe the Drill Instructors Innie Minnie Miney Moe'd us. Nevertheless, the three of us walked outside, with our three Commanding Officers following behind. After reaching a clearing, we got told to stop, then immediately began to get "smoked".

Getting smoked in boot camp is a regular thing which involved doing any and every imaginable exercise with little rest in between. These, again, included sit-ups, leg lifts, push-ups, butterflies, starbursts, running in place or anything else you can think of from the days of high school P.E. class.

Before we got taken outside, I overheard the three DI's make a wager to see who they thought would quit from being smoked first. So at that moment it dawned on me this was simply for their own cruel entertainment.

The three of us recruits immediately dropped and began doing push-ups. We pumped away, pushing until our arms burned and still continued until the cue to flip over onto our backs to begin sit-ups was given. The beating continued for about a half an hour when one of the recruit's legs gave out in the middle of doing squats.

"One down," a DI said to another.

By this point, the floor under me and the other recruit was wet from the sweat dripping from our drenched shirts. My heart was racing. This was one of the hardest physical things I ever had to do. But I would not give in. I had it in my mind that I would die from heat stroke before I quit. The pain and agony was unbearable. It is difficult for me to describe what I was going through; it seemed as if both my body and mind did not want to continue. They didn't believe it would be possible to continue. It was some outside force that kept the repetitions flowing, as if I were transformed into a robot. I don't know how, but I did.

It must have been an hour that had passed before the DI's decided to stop the pounding. I couldn't be happier. Fireworks and champagne bottles were being set off in my mind. It was the excitement of my birthday, the New Year and Halloween all put into one amazing package.

The Drill Instructors had a look of surprise on their face and from then on, I noticed a definite change of attitude they had toward me and the other recruit. I could tell they had gained respect for us.

After that point, the time just flew. Everything else was nothing like the hazing we received. I was also well-liked from then on and didn't have to do the shit jobs others had to do. I was by no means a pet of the DI's, but rather like one of them. And they treated me as such.

The final days of boot camp fast approached. In no time, we were granted liberty for an entire day just before we graduated. This liberty time could be spent doing whatever we wanted, wherever we wanted. But most of the soon-to-be soldiers simply used the time to do a bit of shopping just outside of base, since none of us knew where we were or knew anyone who could supply us with a ride.

I used this time to venture out a bit to the local tattoo parlor with a few other mates. One of our Drill Instructors mentioned a place to get some good work done. He also mentioned that he would get a hefty discount on his next tat if he sent a bunch of his recruits to this parlor. This would be my first tattoo I would get. A few others would follow as the years went by. This first one I decided to get on my upper arm. It hurt, yes, but the pain wasn't unbearable. Nothing much else happened that day, just a lot of relaxing after the tattoo. Everyone was worn out from the previous four months of hard work.

The next morning was not the best cup of coffee I had ever had. Right after our wake up call, the entire platoon stood at attention in front of their racks, or beds, just like any other day.

The quiet morning air was soon interrupted by, "Holy shit! What the fuck is on your arm, recruit?!" a Drill Instructor boasted as he stared at a fresh tattoo on my buddy's forearm.

The question was a rhetorical one and it was followed with a strict command by the same Drill Instructor. Mind you, this was a different DI from the one who recommended us to get tattoos at the shop he knew about.

"Everyone get the fuck outside, shirts off!" the Staff Sergeant yelled out at us.

He didn't have to instruct to remove any pants or shorts, given that we slept with only an undershirt, socks and skivvies. Skivvies just means underwear.

The entire platoon hurried outside and began forming up into ranks.

"I'm writin' every one of you motherfuckers up who decided to go get a tattoo yesterday. You're all getting article 15's," the Drill Instructor said.

He wailed with a brief explanation, "It is against my UCMJ to fuckin' get a goddamn tattoo, goddamn it." He continued his rant, "It's fuckin' destruction of my fuckin' government's property, you fuckin' clowns."

The DI was absolutely correct. It does say in the UCMJ that exact thing, but this rule usually goes unnoticed, being that the majority of military personnel have tattoos. It was an empty threat. None of us were cited with article 15's. I'm sure the reasoning behind it was just to get a good laugh out of smoking us hard one last time before we were to graduate.

A few days later, we became soldiers. We had to celebrate. All platoons that had just graduated received four days of leave before going to airborne school to train how to properly jump out of airplanes without killing one's self.

I got together with about 10 others who were going to go to a nearby lake resort to relax and drink the past four months away. None of these people were from my platoon. I felt a little out of place, but I warmed up to them rather quickly.

We showed up to a cabin right on the lakeside. This thing was huge. It had a massive living room, perfect for all of us to chill in. It had a rustic, yet modern feel to it with up-to-date furniture and drapery all about. Giant windows were all around to create the impression of being right on the lake itself. The empty refrigerator was soon filled with a truckload of beer and liquor. The drinking started before we even stepped foot inside.

I drank as if I was trying to make up for the past four months of not drinking. The whole night was going very well. We were all having a good time, talking, relaxing and messing around. I remember going outside for a cigarette. I saw a golf cart off to the side of the road. These must have been used by the workers at the resort to get around from cabin to cabin, being that there was a handsome amount of space in between each one. The golf cart looked so lonely, so I decided to take it for a quick joy ride. I staggered towards it, giving myself a personal sobriety check by trying to walk a straight line before I sat in the driver's seat. The line I walked was as straight as the cord on an old telephone. So I sat in, turned it over, and set out towards the woods.

I reached the tree line and began to swerve side to side to avoid the closely spaced trees. The gas pedal was constantly floored which made the wheels lose traction on the softer parts of the ground. Visibility was great with the moon shining brightly through the thinned out trees. In an instant, I found myself lying on the floor, about 20 feet away from my ride. It was as if I was driving, blinked, then was face down on the ground.

What the hell happened? I kept asking myself.

I stood upright and dusted off the dirt and leaves that riddled my clothes. In a daze, I looked around to catch a glimpse of the cart. There it stood, about 20 feet away from me with the front bumper caved into a 'v' shape directly behind a pole sticking out of the ground. I wasn't hurt, but rather angry. I was mad at the jerk cart that crashed into this pole. It wasn't me that crashed into it, it was that damn cart.

So I ran over, started it up again and began driving it towards the lake. I approached the water at full speed. Just as I was not more than five feet from the water's edge, I jumped right out of the carriage. The golf cart didn't go very deep into the lake. The water was quick to destroy any momentum it had. Regardless, the club workers had a fun time fishing it out of the lake. That taught that damn cart to crash into things while I was driving it.

I hurried back to the cabin, still furious. I saw a lawn chair outside of another cabin. I decided to now take out my anger on the resort, tossing the lawn chair into the lake. Tables, ashtrays, umbrellas, radios and whatever else got in my way was thrown into either the lake or the resort pool. By the time I reached our cabin, I felt a little better and slept easily that night.

All of us were awoken the next morning to the sound of banging on the front door. The door was answered with the resort manager and two Military Police standing with arms crossed. The manager looked a bit upset for some reason. He was barking at us and at the MP's, saying we destroyed his cabins the previous night and we needed to pay for all the damages caused. He also waved around a piece of paper with a list of the items missing or destroyed. The amount of $2,500 kept coming out of his mouth. That must have been how much I owed.

The Military Police stepped inside and began questioning us as a whole. They found out what platoon we were in and that we had just graduated from basic training. When asked if any of us had done this, we all had blank looks and didn't answer. The resort manager had no actual proof that any one of us took part in the mayhem, but I think he just kind of assumed, since he already knew that we were 10 soldiers who had just graduated from boot camp and hauled a party's worth amount of booze into a single refrigerator the night of. Simple mathematics deduced the culprits to be us.

The MP's weren't getting any information from us. They switched their attention to the manager who was still out of control, screaming like an insane person. The fresh soldiers split up into separate smaller groups to try to quickly find a plan of action and alibi, but I was left to contemplate alone.

After realizing there was no use in trying to calm the rabid manager, the Military Police went back to questioning the soldiers, this time going to each of the smaller groups to find inconsistencies with stories. I was doing my own thing, off in my own world not paying attention to each conversation. It was still too early for me.

After interrogating some of the others, one of the MP's came up to me and asked, "You're Stiles, right?"

"Yeah," I replied back to him, surprised he had remembered my name from the brief introduction we gave earlier.

"Man, these other guys over here are tryin' to pin this whole thing on you," he honestly said to me. "It sounds like they want to skate out of this and let you take the heat for it all."

It was noble and cool that the MP gave me a head's up about what was supposed to go down. While they were correct, the others still had no right to blame me because they had no idea what had happened the night before.

There was no way I was going to pay $2,500. At the first clear opportunity I saw, I slipped out of the cabin and got out of there as stealthily and quickly as I could. I was still able to hear the screams and yells of the angry owner as I weaved myself in and out of the trees toward the main highway.

I never found out what happened after that with the debt that I incurred. Maybe the others had to pay; maybe the manager had it in his heart to let it slide that one time. My guess is that it was the former.

Chapter Five

As much as I disliked airborne school, I was able to pass through the short course. I have always been afraid of heights and that's just something I don't think I will ever conquer. That fact is what made airborne school extremely difficult. We were doing jumps from only a couple thousand feet off the ground which gave us little time to ensure a proper landing. I came scarily close to breaking my legs on more than one occasion. I could not get over the fear of mishap while falling freely out of the sky. But I needed to push through the prerequisite so I could begin the sole reason for joining the Army: Ranger school. My persistence prevailed and I was off to RIP, Ranger Indoctrination Program.

The program was at the same Army base as airborne school, so it was a short march over to the headquarters. It turned out that I joined RIP at the perfect time: the instructors for the course were about to begin a two week leaving period, which meant we basically had to go on a two week leave as well. We couldn't begin the course without any instructors, and the Army wasn't going to send a different group of instructors just for the two weeks that the originals were to be missing. Right away I booked a flight back home to see some friends. I was to leave in two days, just enough time for me to tidy myself up and look like a proper soldier for the flight home. A drive uptown to an outlet store named Ranger Joe's to pick up some jump boots was all I really needed.

The next day, I wanted to check out a movie at the theater just outside of base, and then I would be on my way to grab my boots. The movie I walked into was called "The Loser". The star of the movie is Jason Biggs. With the success of his previous movie, "American Pie", I thought his follow up would be worth checking out.

The movie was the biggest flop I had ever seen. It was such a big upset that I just left without finishing the movie. I couldn't stand it.

I walked outside the movie theater and coincidentally saw another two soldiers from the RIP program, Private Roost and Private Heshman.

"What's up guys? What are you up to?" I asked them.

"Nothin' much. We're about to head up to Victoria Drive," Roost answered.

Victoria Drive is a very popular hangout spot for the local soldiers. They spend time there to do shopping, find girls or eat some tasty food after MRE's become tiresome.

Meals Ready to Eat are the staple foods for when a company is out on a field mission and don't have the luxury of eating a proper meal.

"Cool, man. You guys care if I roll with you?" I asked them. "I'm headed the same way. We can share a cab up there and you can drop me off at Ranger Joe's."

"Yeah, let's go," Roost replied.

We caught the first cab we saw and directed the driver toward where we needed to go.

We were almost to Ranger Joe's when Heshman told the cab driver to stop. The driver pulled over to the side of the road, just outside a hotel parking lot.

The three of us hopped out as Heshman said to me, "We gotta take care of something real quick, cool?"

The question didn't need an answer.

We started walking towards the hotel, and more specifically, towards the bar entrance of the hotel. Heshman opened the door for us and we walked inside as he made a hello gesture to the cute bartender. We pulled up a stool and Heshman began talking to this chick in a sort of low manner, as if he was pulling a drug deal. This entire time the girl had a confused look on her face, as if she was trying to solve the answer to a riddle. It looked to me as if she recognized us from somewhere and she was trying to figure out from where.

"We're tryin' to pick up some rocks," Roost said to the girl.

"Yeah?" she answered. "You got what I want?"

Roost pulled out and laid a few twenty dollar bills on the table. The girl swiped the money and headed over to the side of the bar where the well liquor was. She began to make a mixed drink, probably for an order she had just received, when the look of epiphany came across her face. She finally got it. She now knew where she had seen us before.

The bartender slid the mixed drink she just created to the far end of the bar top, rang a bell, and walked toward a table where customers dine. She reached a table where a lone gentleman sat. All three of our stomachs hit rock bottom at that point. The man that was sitting at the table was a cadre for the RIP program. Cadre is an inflated word to describe someone in charge. We stood out of our stools and headed for the door. But it was too late, the chick had already pointed us out and the cadre jumped out of his table and headed right for us. The girl obviously told him what was about to go down. These two clowns were about to buy some crack cocaine. They were willing to risk it all, just a few weeks after basic training.

"Jesus fucking Christ, why didn't you guys tell me what you were doing!?" I yelled out at them. "You could have just dropped me off first then come back!"

"It's done!" Heshman exclaimed. "Let's just try to get the fuck out of here!"

As soon as our feet stepped outside, we began to run with hopes of escaping the pursuit.

It only took about four seconds to hear the cadre yell out, "Soldiers! Get your asses the fuck over here!"

If this was any other time, I would have just kept on running and been out of the woods. But this is where the brainwashing of boot camp showed itself as all three of us came to a complete stop, turned around in defeat, and walked back to the instructor.

"I know what the fuck you three were up to," he began. "Get the fuck to post and wait for me there. I'm gonna fuckin' have a field day on your asses."

I was thinking to myself this was the last day of my Army career. For sure I was going to get kicked out. But then again, I didn't do anything wrong. I don't do crack, I hadn't done any drugs since I had been in the Army. I should be in the clear. I was only an innocent bystander in that whole mess. This should be a piece of cake to talk myself out of, I thought. I definitely have a way with words and I knew I would be able to use them to my advantage for this.

The cadre went back into the bar, probably to finish his drink and to get all the information the bartender knew about us.

"Let's head back to base like he told us and wait for him," I said to both Private Roost and Private Heshman.

"Nah, dude. We're gettin' the fuck out of here," Roost replied back to me.

"Dude, he told us to wait for him back at post," I told him with false concern. Secretly I was hoping that they wouldn't show up just to build up my case for release.

I continued, "Whatever. I'm goin' back to base to wait for him. You guys do whatever the hell you want."

And I did just that. I went to the headquarters of the Ranger school and waited. I must have waited a good two hours. The cadre never showed up; neither did Roost nor Heshman.

The next day, after waking up at the barracks, I was called into the office of the cadre. I quickly threw on my daily fatigue uniform and rushed into the office, the whole time thinking about what I was going to say to convince him that I shouldn't be kicked out of the service. I walked into the office and stood at ease until the order to sit was given.

"Sit the fuck down," the cadre said. I made out the last name of Roberts stitched on his perfectly ironed uniform. His collar boasted a pin with three chevrons and one rocker, which annotated his Staff Sergeant rank.

I took a seat and he began to announce my demise.

"I fuckin' know what you guys were doing there," Staff Sergeant Roberts said. "That bartender you were trying to get crack off of is my fuckin' sister."

No wonder why she ratted us out.

"Staff Sergeant, I was only sharing a ride with those other two guys," my rebuttal started. "I was heading up to Ranger Joe's to pick up some jump boots for the leave back home and was supposed to just be sharing a ride. These other guys are the ones that are into that kind of stuff."

"How the fuck am I supposed to believe that?" he said, unconvinced. "I just had Private Roost and Private Heshman in here 10 minutes ago saying you were all involved. Now who the fuck am I supposed to believe?"

Those jerks told on my ass. Fucking shit. As soon as someone messes with me, I'm going to mess them up.

"What? That's not true, Staff Sergeant," I said. "If you piss test us right now, I guarantee you those two will pop and I'll run clean."

"That's a fuckin' great idea, Private Stiles," he told me. "I'm gonna fuckin' piss test you this afternoon. As of right now, the three of you are getting Article 15's. The fuckin' three of you have seven days extra duty and seven days restriction to the barracks. This means no leave for you motherfuckers."

"Oh, and guess what," he added. "No more Ranger school for either of you."

Ouch. That was a sharp dagger through my heart. Becoming a Ranger was why I joined the service. It would have allowed me to be the efficient killer I had always wanted to be. My life's dream was shattered in an instant. Jesus Christ.

This was a big turning point in my life. I can say with almost definite certainty that if I had gotten into the Ranger school, I would still be in the Army today, pursuing the highest possible Special Force possible. Today, I would have probably been in the Delta Force. No chance of that happening since that day.

The urinalysis was taken by the three of us later that unforgettable day. I had nothing to worry about. I already knew what my result would be.

The next day, Roost and Heshman began their out-processing paperwork. They popped positive and I was glad. Those fuckers cost me my Ranger school. Those fuckers made the start of my Army career a terrible one.

Chapter Six

The life that I led before the police force prepared me well enough to deal with anything that a common civilian would throw at me in the line of duty. Army life was much more difficult and required more attention than most other jobs out there. We were taught how to survive through all types of hardships. Those hardships could have been anything war would introduce to us to anything Nature would have us go through. Both of these were formidable enemies and I would have a hard time discussing which was the most potent. Nature did once have a hold onto what I thought was my life, though.

After being kicked from Ranger school, I was sent to my home base in Washington State. Fort Lewis to be exact. This was where I would spend the rest of my four years in service, and a hell of four years they were.

Washington was very different from what I was used to: there are lots of forest areas right next to deserts, many open roads, no lights on some paved roads, lots of open space and not to mention the weather. It only took about three weeks for me to appreciate the power of Nature and Washington's extreme weather.

I was on a field problem. A field problem is basically like a mission soldiers must perform out in the field, away from an actual base, real or not. This particular field problem called for us to ambush a massive deuce and a half army truck about 20 clicks (kilometers) from base camp. It was a fairly simple operation. It required little effort and expertise as well as few supplies. After the ambush, we would simply head back to camp.

We had started our 20 kilometer walk through the Yakama desert shortly after receiving our warning order, at about four in the afternoon. The warning order gives instructions as to what to do out in the field. We didn't pack very much. Our canteens, light ammunition and arms and light backpacks with simple items, such as MRE's, gloves or an extra cap went with us. Our woobies weren't even taken, which proved to be a massive mistake. Woobies are small blankets made out of light material. We weren't to make any stops during this whole process, so there really wasn't a need for them—at least we thought.

The walk was easy. It wasn't too strenuous to the point where we were struggling, but strenuous enough for us to keep warm in the diving temperatures. There was little formation, our Sergeant Platoon Leader was really laid back and didn't care about formalities. It was basically just a few hours of 'shootin' the shit'—talking about whatever came to mind.

The cold started making itself apparent after midnight. We did our best to do whatever it took to keep warm. We would run around in circles as we marched, stop and do push-ups or anything else that required us to exert ourselves more than just walking. This was the desert at the beginning of winter. I'm from southern California. The coldest it gets in my hometown is just barely low enough to frost up my windows early in the morning.

Midnight slowly rolled over. The night began to feel like it was crawling by. If only the moon could reflect just one degree more of the sun's energy, that would have made such a big difference. I don't think it would have been so bad if there wasn't any wind blowing. But an arctic desert wind made my face numb. My colleagues pointed out tears running down my face from the blowing wind without me even feeling them staggering past my nostrils. The gloves I wore made little difference. Cigarettes weren't even staying properly lit in the freezing weather. The entire platoon trudged forward, heads down, desperately looking forward to seeing the ten-ton iron deuce and a half driving by so we can make our ambush and hurry back to base camp.

Our stopping point had finally arrived, at the top of a short hill, at about half past one o'clock in the morning. 'Prior intelligence' told us that the rendezvous would shortly occur. But it didn't . . .

An hour had passed. It was obvious the deuce was not going to show. Winds must have been up to at least 20 miles per hour, at the top of that bulge. The entire platoon lay close together to share what warmth was left from one another. Some soldiers from the squad lay 'nut to butt' on the unsettling dirt floor, which was basically the spoon position, only this was the least sexy occasion for such a sight. It was getting late and we were all very tired, but fuck it was cold. We did our best to catch a resting eye.

My body felt unlike anything it had felt before. There was a very odd sensation coursing through my system. The feeling crept quickly through my body, starting from my extremities and flowing inward like multiple shots of heroin finding their way to my core being. Everything about my body was turning cold and my breathing slowed to a forced stagger. I can't exactly explain it, but it was as if I had lost feeling in most of my limbs but was able to feel blood trying to work its way to these lost parts of my body. The numbness allowed for little suffering. Tingling sensations danced all about. I honestly thought I was about to die.

"Sergeant," I began to say to my platoon leader. "It's fuckin' cold out here. I have never felt like this before in my life."

"We all feel like this, Stiles," my sergeant replied. "Just try to get some sleep. We'll be out of here soon."

I don't know how I did it, but my impending death was masked and treated with a couple hours of sleep.

It was about six o'clock in the morning when I was awoken by my platoon sergeant. "Let's get our gear together and get the fuck back to base," he told us all.

I tried standing up, but it was difficult to do while not able to feel neither my feet nor my hands.

My limbs were numb, and my toes actually still have no feeling associated with them to this day. Trying to move around was a bit difficult. It was as if I were a one year old child taking its first steps. I tottered toward my gear and tried to pick it all up with the now stubs as hands. In my clumsiness, I knocked over my canteen. It fell to the ground and hit a nearby rock. A high pitched clank resulted from the canteen hitting the rock. A bit unusual, I thought. Without the help of my useless fingers, I twisted the cap of my canteen open with both my palms to have a look inside. Sure enough, the water inside had been frozen solid.

The entire platoon staggered back, looking totally defeated.

This conquered feeling was our own fault. We should have been more prepared for what was out there.

The more and more time I spent in the service I realized this kind of shit happened quite often. Missions and objectives were repeatedly made more difficult than they actually needed to be due to lack of communication or intelligence. I soon learned to be ready for anything. And it was with this teaching that I am able to tolerate a lot of shit.

At the sheriff's station not too long ago, I was talking to a cop about living conditions the both of us had in the past. The topic of where and how we lived somehow came up. He kept going on and on about how when he had first moved into his current apartment he was unable to get proper sleep for a week until he bought window blinds.

"Yeah, man, every goddamn morning I would wake up at 6 o'clock," he clamored. "The sun shined right in my eyes! How the fuck am I supposed to sleep through that?!"

Sun in your fucking eyes? I thought, Jesus Christ, this guy was in a warm comfortable bed and he was complaining that a little sunlight in his eyes was disturbing his dreams of pink bunny rabbits sitting around a table sipping some tea with jolly mister pig and sleepy cat. Holy fuck . . . Try sleeping outside every night for a month with heavy gunfire sounding off constantly. Try sleeping in below freezing weather with only the clothes on your back to provide warmth. Try not sleeping for days on end. Once a person has done these things, then they are allowed to complain.

Chapter Seven

I quickly and easily grew comfortable with life in Washington and with life serving in the Army. Showing up to work every morning, every now and then proving you can still run a mile, knocking off a field problem here and there and being on the look-out for drug tests was all it took to get through the Army with an honorable discharge. Sounds pretty simple, right? For me, it was. But to be honest, there were times when it seemed as if all my friends were being knocked out one by one because of drugs. They were dropping like flies at one point. They didn't have the right connections like I did. I had a sergeant on the inside let me know in advance when a drug test was to be given the following week.

The military says the tests are given at random, but that's not really the case. And not everybody knows these drug tests are usually done to only check for a certain type of drug, rather than checking for all types. Checking all known drugs or even just the most common drugs is quite costly, and even the government needs to be stingy sometimes. This inside information proved extremely helpful to me after one weekend of pill-related happiness. I didn't actually get tested myself, but that entire day I had lime-green urine because of some over-the-counter vial ingestion used to ward off the scent of drugs in one's urine.

Drugs became a normal part of my life with this new relaxed, almost cocky relationship with the Army. They not only became a normal part of my life, but they were used quite frequently after the discovery of a nearby rave that hosted a party every weekend. Anyone who says that ecstasy doesn't make a rave better by tenfold is lying to you like Clinton lied to the American public. Every pounding note is not only heard, but felt in a way that brings the same smile and happiness to one's face as a child's on a Christmas morning. The reverberations can easily be considered aphrodisiacs. And if that's not enough of a push for the illegal stuff, just think of all the stories that can be an added bonus to the wonderful feelings brought to you by such a simple substance.

One Saturday night, which started out just like any other, I found myself at the rave. Let's just give it the name 'Keen' for now. I was with my girlfriend at the time. Let's call her 'Sophia'. We were there along with one of my good Army friends. Hell, since we're just throwing names around, let's call him 'Job'.

A bit of background information on Job: this guy was a stud. He was tall and ripped with venous muscles. His smooth tongue had its way with the ladies, and I'm sure not with just the lyrical content.

Job had women all around him all the time, as if he were constantly on a Beijing subway during rush hour. He had unsatisfactory flowing hair on top of an artist's depiction of a Greek God. Both men and women fell in love with his soft blue eyes and starry smile. His Army uniform was not needed to help him get laid.

The three of us took a few pills together before we entered the rave, and Job added some weed to the mix. Once inside, Sophia and I wandered off to enjoy one another while on ecstasy. Job went on his own, surely to pick up a little sweetheart for the night. He was a big boy and was able to take care of himself.

Sophia and I got tired fairly quick as the night went on, probably because we only had a soft buzz compared to what we were used to. So we decided to spend the rest of the night at home with a few drinks in hand. We set off through the crowds of people to search for Job.

It didn't take us long to spot him from afar with his tongue down someone's throat. I gave my eyes a sturdy rub after I saw Job. I thought my mind was playing tricks on me. It wasn't that I was unsure whether or not it was Job, but was more of a want—no, need—for clarification about who he was with. I didn't want to accept it; this couldn't be true. Sophia and I looked at one another, and then looked at Job. Again, we looked at one another, and then looked at Job. He wasn't with a really ugly girl that would make Beethoven hurl into his piano, no. He wasn't with a massive girl big enough to affect the tides, no. His lips and tongue were wrapped around another man's. I mean, this wasn't a transvestite or a guy who could get confused for a girl. This was a man. This was a man who looked like a man, and who had a penis like a man. Hairy knuckles flowing through two men's hair is no sight to be witnessed.

I looked at Sophia and exploded with laughter.

It took a good 30 seconds for me to yell out, "Holy fuck! What the hell is Job doing with that guy?" I rhetorically asked Sophia. "He's fuckin' makin' out with another dude!" My laughter continued.

Staring at Job and his partner with a disgusted look, Sophia asked me, "What the fuck is going on?! Why is Job kissing that guy?!"

We knew the obvious answer. When a person is high, there's no telling what will happen. It was unfortunate to Job that he gave us a front row seat to this phenomenon.

The only explanation Job could give to Sophia and me the next day was, "Dude, I was high. I didn't know what the hell I was doing."

On a separate occasion, it was the lack of ecstasy which caused me to go sleepless for 2 days straight just before a week-long field problem. We usually went to Keen prepared with all the essential pharmaceutical items, but on this particular night, Sophia, Job and I were blindly counting on one another to bring a small supply for the group. This didn't go as planned as we were now stranded dry. We looked at each other with the same disappointed look as we were all thinking how we couldn't go through this night sober.

I gave Sophia a small nudge on the arm, gave her a nod of my head and said, "Hey, go around and try to find us some 'E'."

Of course, 'E' is one of the street terms for ecstasy, not only because it's the first letter in the original word, but it is also used to stand for 'emotion'. The MDMA part of ecstasy pills taps into any emotion the user is experiencing at that moment and amplifies it, which is why it is well-known that having sex while 'rolling' on ecstasy is incomparable to anything of the like. Love, relationships, spiritual feelings and imagination are just some of the possible areas affected by the drug.

To me and many others, ecstasy is a wonderful drug that can bring out amazing, unimaginable experiences never known to be possible by the human mind. Those who think ecstasy is a harmful and bad drug simply don't have all the facts. A rare death 'after ingesting ecstasy' seen on a local newscast of a senior student in high school with goals and ambitions in life set to become reality after taking up a fully paid scholarship to Ivy League University of Pennsylvania have people frightened of the possibilities. I am extremely confident the cause of death from cases like the above is from a foreign substance the ecstasy pill was laced with. It is not uncommon to find methamphetamines or heroin strewn in the mix of the tablets. Those are just bad pills and unfortunately they have given a great drug a bad name.

Being a beautiful and out-spoken individual, Sophia wasn't shy and never had any trouble meeting new people. She is tall and confident with every step she takes. Her eyes are bold with a seriousness that would turn any weak bull into a cow. Her Nordic ancestry gave her the right cushioning in the right areas, but she was far from overweight. Sophia was very much picturesque, given the correct makeup and attitude. She has always had long hair but the same certainty can't be said for the color. At the time of this past rave, I remember it being pitch black, almost too black to the point where it turns purple.

Sophia walked around the partygoers, on a mission to acquire some goods. Surrounding her were swaying bodies with shut eyes. The only visible life in these zombies was the closed smile and gentle bobbing of their heads. She would sometimes bump into one after trying to avoid the spastic arms of what seemed to be wacky waving inflatable arm flailing tube men and women. It didn't take long to find a friend who was also a supplier.

After a quick greeting with long time friend 'V-dub', Sophia asked him, "Hey man, you got any 'x' for me and some friends?"

"Fuckin' a, Sophia. Demand is high for that shit," he said. "I'm fresh out of the cheap shit, doll, but I might be able to help you out with some of this crazy shit."

V-dub reached into his jacket breast pocket and pulled out a roll of pills that looked like something you would find at the check-out counter of a grocery store. Who knows, maybe that's where he got them.

The name 'V-dub' came early in his life to steer clear from any bullying during his school years with the real given name of Voight Wasserman. Not the coolest sounding name, but his parents are the ones to blame.

He handed over the roll to Sophia and told her, "Try this shit. They call 'em Rolls Royce's." He continued, "High-end shit, Soph. You'll be trippin' your balls off, you'll see."

The smile on V-dub's face wasn't the slightest reassuring to Sophia. Nothing about this situation seemed legitimate. Sophia stared at him with an unconvinced face.

"V, what the fuck is this?" she asked, holding up the roll.

"Don't fret, yo," V-dub tried to put Sophia at ease. "You're goin' to be thankin' me tomorrow. Now get your pretty ass out of here."

He turned Sophia around and gave her a slight push on the back.

Sophia made her way back to me and Job and handed me the roll of pills.

"Here, you guys," she began telling us. "I got these from a friend but he was acting real shady 'n shit. I don't know what the hell they are."

With no hesitation, Job reached for three pills and said, "I don't give a fuck what they are. I'll let you know what happens."

Job popped the pills and headed over to the dance floor to begin having a heart attack. Nothing was actually the matter. Medically speaking, nothing was actually the matter. Job just can't dance . . .

Sophia looked at me and said, "I'm not takin' those things. Are you gonna take 'em?" she questioned me.

"I don't know, man," I started telling her. "I wanna see what happens with Job first, then if everything seems cool, I'll have a couple."

This whole incident was going on as I was still getting introduced to the variety of drugs that are out there. I was still uneasy every time I experimented with something new. I'm no idiot. I still want to know at least a little bit about what might happen while intoxicated before I actually take a substance. But there are some things that happen after ingestion that I hate to claim responsibility for.

After about 20 minutes of watching Job writhe in pain on the dance floor, I went over to him and pulled him aside.

"Hey dude, how are you feelin'?" I asked Job as his body slowly ceased to dance.

Sophia joined us at the outer ring of the rave.

"I'm feelin' good, man," Job replied back to me. "Everything's cool, a bit tingly, but cool. You should really try some of that stuff," he told me.

"I don't know, dude, you think so?" I tried not to let my paranoia emanate.

"It looks like Job's doin' all right," Sophia said. "I'll be here, anyway, to take care of you if something happens."

Hesitantly, I reached into my pocket and grabbed two pills.

"Okay, here goes," I said to Sophia and Job.

I popped them and tried to relax. Even though I knew pills took a few minutes to have the effects start to be noticed, I expected something to happen right away. I guess I just really wanted to know what these things truly were and if this was a good idea or bad idea.

Not two minutes after I took the drugs, Job's face quickly turned awry. I knew right away he wasn't joking, either.

"Dude, I feel weird," he said to me.

"Aww, shit, man. Don't tell me that," I said back to him. "I'm not in the mood to hear something like that right now."

My mind flew in all different directions. My thoughts alone were making this the most potent drug I have ever had, turning nothing into something. The unknown of what would happen next had me breathing heavier than normal, worried. This was the placebo effect to the extreme in the wrong way intended.

I sat down on the sticky floor and wrapped my arms around my raised knees. I tried to keep a cool and calm mind, but it seemed like it was impossible at that time. It was a good thing to have Sophia there to slap some sense into me if I needed it. And that's exactly what she did. For two days straight.

Within those two days were weird visions and feelings. I remember seeing a beautiful leprechaun girl with curly red hair carrying a basket. She was simply skipping along, minding her own business.

Those two days were also void of any sleep whatsoever. The lack of sleep played a brutal toll on my body when I had a five day field problem immediately following the dancing pumpkin visions in my mind.

Sophia later found out exactly what those pills were that we took. It definitely wasn't ecstasy, but instead was dextromethorphan, or DXM for short. DXM is a cough suppressant found in most over-the-counter cold medicines. When taken in higher amounts, it can act as a hallucinogen. Some teenagers find themselves spending a lot of time at the over-the-counter aisle at the local supermarket for this exact reason. That, along with my paranoia, is what kept my mind flowing with restlessness.

Chapter Eight

Emotions were bouncing off the walls, hitting everything in their path like a loose mechanical bull on the morning of September 11, 2001. I obviously don't need to go into details here, that day is already in the history books. If you asked anyone how or what they were feeling on that day you would have gotten mixed responses. Some people might have said they were scared that the two plane hijackings were only the precursor to something bigger that would cause the destruction of the world. Others might have said they were angry at those who were responsible for doing such a thing and they felt as if retaliation was a definite next move for the United States. Some people were even confused at the whole situation, not wanting to accept reality. And, of course, some people experienced all of these emotions within a short period of time.

Any normal person, especially those living in the United States, would have had an emotion like the ones above coursing through their veins. But *none* of the above was going through my mind on that unforgettable day. Excitement would have described my feeling. I feel as if I am repeating myself when I ask you to not look at me as a lunatic, but to be honest, I wasn't the only one to feel that way.

This may sound odd to some, but if you asked the United States Army Infantrymen what feeling they had on September 11, 2001, the majority of them would have an answer very similar to mine. These are people trained to fight in combat, trained to kill. They have spent years practicing war-time tactics in their homeland with details spared because those details can only be seen on real front lines. The ammunition used is real, most of the time, but targets and terrain can only be mimicked. This day of reckoning was the excuse for soldiers to finally use what they had learned, to take the ultimate test. Military barracks were turned into party frat houses.

Shortly after the collapse of the Twin Towers in New York, I found myself drunk with not only excitement, but with a case of beers I had just inhaled in my barracks room with some friends. It was a time of celebration for us. Drunken lullabies were being tossed about the way sailors would do around a feast of grog on the night before a long-awaited port call. The couple of days prior were like an extended New Year's Eve party. War wasn't to be declared for another 18 months, but we were acting as if we would be set out on the following morning. The festivities continued until our secret sauce was tapped.

"Yo, Stiles, we're out of beer," I heard a voice cry out. "Grab the reins and fly!"

I was the only one in my tight group of friends that actually had a form of transportation while in Fort Lewis. Just before my first day in the base, I made a quick stop down in California to pick up my 1995 Pontiac Firebird. I loved my ride. It was sleek black with chromed 20 inch rims. The 300 standard V8 ponies were boosted with a custom exhaust, an engine cooling unit, headers and cold air intake. This was my baby, although I didn't treat it as such. I loved this car to death, but man, I wasn't going to take the time out of my day to wash it!

With everyone else's cars or motorcycles back in their hometowns, I didn't mind running errands every now and then to take care of my friends.

I grabbed my keys and set out to grab a few more cases of beer. I walked out of the room and out of the barracks towards my car in the dusty, rocky parking lot on the side of the building. The ride to the PX was only about 5 minutes and I wasn't even drunk to the point where it would affect my driving. I opened the door to my Firebird, turned over the engine and sped off a bit faster, more reckless and louder than usual. Dust and debris spit up behind me as the tires of my car couldn't quite keep traction.

About 30 minutes had passed before I returned to the parking lot with the beer. I parked my car and sat in the driver's seat for a few seconds. I saw two Military Police officers eying me. I left the cases of beer in the car and began to walk to the barracks.

"Is that your vehicle?" one of the officers asked me, pointing to my Firebird.

"Well, it all depends on what's goin' on," I smartly replied to him.

They replied back to me, even smarter, "Turn around and put your hands behind your back, private."

"Whoa, dude, you arrest soldiers for mouthing off to cops now?" my cockiness continued.

I complied with the officer and got myself ready to be under arrest. In a short distance, I could hear a female hollering towards me and the MP's. I looked toward the commotion and saw an African American fat ass female pointing her chicken leg stubbed fingers in my direction and yelling out obscenities that I tried to decipher by just reading her lips. Just looking at this sea cow made me clench my fists and squint my eyes with hatred. It was obvious she was pointing me out from the short police line-up that consisted of just me. But this victim wasn't behind a two-way mirror, sobbing in almost silence. This was quite the opposite.

"We have a complaint that you purposely spit up rocks and dirt onto the private property of a vehicle that is not yours," one of the officers said to me as he fastened a set of handcuffs around my wrists.

A scene was beginning to form and soldiers from different barracks were coming out to see what was going on. I saw my roommate Duncan heading over to where the screaming behemoth stood. We all called him 'Dirty Duncan' for reasons that were easily apparent at first sight of the man.

Dirty was born and raised in the southern United States. When one thinks of someone from the south, images of pale, thin, ripped shirt and tattered pants wearing specimens come to mind. This was Duncan. He had a film of dirt and filth over his body at all times. At least this is how it seemed, much like Linus from the Peanuts gang. His hair was always a mess and he cared little about his health or image. Dirty smoked at least two packs of cigarettes every day, which added to his grubby appearance and gave him a second nickname of 'grimy'.

Grimy had later found himself in trouble with the Army when he got caught smoking marijuana while enlisted. The military has a zero tolerance policy for drugs so paperwork for Duncan's way out of the Army quickly started after the discovery of THC in his urine. But before the final processing could be finished, Grimy had the idea to go AWOL. This is Absence Without Leave, which means he basically fled as a military fugitive, trying to avoid a negative discharge.

A few months after his unauthorized absence (which is what the Naval branch calls it), I managed to see Duncan for one last time. It turned out he got caught by civilian police officers and arrested for rape in a different state. His named was flagged for all governmental authorities to release him back over to Fort Lewis ever since he deserted the Army. While back in Washington, his out processing was commenced and he was chaptered out of the Army.

I saw Duncan over trying to calm the woman who claimed I defiled her car with a stone rain from my reckless driving.

"Yo, try to calm down, relax," Duncan told the woman.

"That motha fucka destroyed my car!" she yelled back at Dirty. "He's gonna pay for all damages! I want my money!"

"Is that your car?" Grimy asked the female, pointing to a dark blue Toyota Corolla they were standing next to.

"Yeah that's my car, nigga," the woman boasted. "It's a fuckin' mess!"

"Here, man, I'll give you 10 bucks to go have the dust washed off of it," Duncan offered. "That's all that's wrong with your damn car. I see no damage whatsoever, bitch."

In all cases where someone is accused of doing harm to another person or their property, the aforementioned is guilty until proven innocent.

I was taken to the main Military Police station and quickly given a breathalyzer test.

There is a sure-fire way to lower a breathalyzer reading by about 10%. If a person hyperventilates just before blowing into the machine, the test results will show a slightly lower reading than if taken normally. But this information was found out too late for me as I blew a .10 reading. The legal limit in the state of Washington is .08. I was underage, anyway, so regardless of the result, I was in trouble.

I immediately got written up with an Article 15 for underage drinking, which required me to be restricted to my barracks with extra duty and reduced pay for 14 days. They also charged me with a DUI.

"Private, you're getting a DUI charge for driving while intoxicated," the Staff Sergeant MP explained to me.

"Staff Sergeant, I wasn't even driving my car," I tried to play it off to avoid the more serious charge.

"My girlfriend was driving; I was in the passenger seat."

"This is going to be taken to civilian court," the MP told me. "Don't try to plead with me; you'll have your chance with a judge."

Fuck, I thought. I don't want to have a driving under the influence charge on my record. That's some serious shit. I didn't want to go through my life with an untrained monkey leaping back and forth between my shoulders. How am I going to get myself out of this one? I'm going to have to put on some extra charm.

Two weeks had passed and I met my DUI case in court after working in the field. I tried to look presentable, dressing in a collared shirt and slacks. I was hoping this would fool the judge into thinking I could never do such an unthinkable act. I brought my wit and 'A-game' with me. I had an eloquent way of making the situation seem as if I never actually drove my car anywhere. The idea was to try to convince the judge I was simply outside testing my new exhaust I had supposedly installed. Besides, the charge in question was DUI, not destruction of property or disorderly conduct. I just had to prove I wasn't driving.

Court was adjourned and the judge sat on his throne to begin reading the report the MP's wrote up. Everyone in the room, including myself, sat in silence, waiting for the judge to make the first move.

The judge was an older man. Hearty meals from the past 50 years or so were catching up to him. His balding head and thin glasses made him look wise and full of knowledge. I imagined that every word spewed from his mouth would be words of wisdom, good enough to be in any book of philosophical theories. He was clean shaven and looked very professional with his garb draping all around him.

He sat, adjusting his glasses every now and again as he continued to read the case against me. His face clenched occasionally as he tried to understand exactly what was going on in the report, as if he was putting himself directly in the front line of the situation. Not only that, but I was sure he was trying to see the circumstance from all possible view points. This man looked as if he were definitely capable of doing such.

After a few moments, he finally announced to me, "Soldier, it seems as if you were apprehended and charge with a DUI outside the barracks where you reside." He continued with the simple question for me to answer, "Is this correct?"

"Yes, sir," I began to say. "I was in my room celebrating and drinking with a few friends and then stepped out to smoke a cigarette."

I continued to explain, "I then saw this woman furious over something that had happened sometime before I stepped outside."

The judge stepped in for clarification and said, "So you got arrested and charged with a driving under the influence charge while you were outside of your barracks smoking a cigarette."

"Yes, sir, that's what went down," I confirmed his statement.

"Private, I'm throwing this case out as well as the charge against you," the judge said to me. "This case makes no sense and you're not going to suffer from it."

With a smile on my face, I gave a relieved thank you to the judge.

"This case is dismissed from the record," the judge announced to everyone in the courtroom. A quick pause in the air then the judge finished with, "And soldier, drink responsibly."

This was surely reference to the fact I was underage and he wanted to give me a simple heed of warning as well as a final thought of circumstantial understanding. The union was not officially in the midst of war, but it sure felt that way at the time. For a 19 year old who may be sent to die defending his country but not be able to legally drink in his country of origin was rather silly. And the judge was fully aware of this.

Soldiers and sailors sometimes get a bad reputation for some of the things they do. But civilians occasionally forget exactly why we have these brave individuals. Their jobs require them to get put through hell because one day they just might be set in that exact situation in another country, away from their friends and families. These rogues are there to protect a nation. They are pulled from the normal society and trained to possibly die for their country. Underneath a hardened exterior, if you ask any young soldier if they have any weaknesses, what lies beneath is a feeling of solitude and uncertainty.

Later in my military career a Staff Sergeant told me a story. He explained how pilots of various rotary aircraft like the Black Hawk and Warrior must fly often to keep their qualifications up-to-date, regardless of war-time or not. The helicopters would roar at different hours of the day in formations and mock-operations would be performed at Army Air Bases, like the one in Alabama. Civilians from neighborhoods close to where flight operations are held were constantly calling the base's commanding officers complaining about the noise and unsettling atmosphere the helos were creating. These complaints were all occurring prior to September 11, 2001. But the phones immediately stopped ringing with complaint after that day. I guess people need to be reminded every now and then exactly why the United States conducts training operations on the homeland. It is a shame this reminder in particular came with lives lost.

Chapter Nine

One of my best friends in the Army was named Ray. Ray was a short Asian guy who had no shame whatsoever. I never knew his exact heritage, where he came from, but my guess would be the Philippines. He had dark skin, but not as dark as most Indonesian's. People from northern parts of Asia, like China and Korea could have a dark skin tone, as well, but Ray's was a bit darker than that. So that would put him in the middle, with the Philippines. Again, this was just a guess. He had thin, dark hair that he spiked when he felt it was necessary. He wasn't only short, but he was also skinny. He was a small guy, but he definitely was not afraid to get into a bar fight. Ray wasn't afraid of anything. He would talk trash to a 210 pound line backer even if he knew it would send him to the hospital shortly thereafter.

I spent a lot of time going out to bars with Ray to pick up girls. His confidence helped out immensely and I thank him for getting the hook up started with some beautiful ladies. The way it usually went was he would approach a group of girls and start up a clever chat to get them interested. After the thin ice was easily broken, I would choose one of the girls to charm for myself. With both our wit, it was a piece of cheesecake to get these girls out of the cold streets and into a hotel room where we would discuss global warming and its effects on the endangered polar bear. Well, it didn't go *exactly* like that, but most of it is true. If the mood was right, I would slip the girls one simple line that worked every time: 'I'm not the kind of guy who sleeps around, but, I just wanna eat you out.' The light would flicker for less than a second and the girl would be bottomless with the return.

On a routine night with Ray, I found myself in a dorm room of a college student after meeting her at a local bar. We were both a bit buzzed from the beers before so things were looking good. This girl was looking beautiful from the moment I saw her, the beers had little effect to make her even more appealing. It wasn't needed. She had long, smooth light brown hair that grazed the small of her back. She wore only a little makeup, like eyeliner, lip gloss and a thin layer of powder from a compact applicator. This girl was just lovely with her bulbous cheeks and d bra size. She had a nice ass, too; plenty to grab on to. Because of all the added fluffiness, I'll admit she was slightly above average in weight. But she wasn't fat.

We made our way to her bedroom and ultimately her bed. Right away, we began to kiss one another with passion, the type of passion two people who have just met have. Tongues were interlocking and spit was not confined to the owner's mouths. I placed my right hand on the side of her face to cradle it. My left hand reached deep into her hair and gave a firm tug. I have always enjoyed pulling hair and this makes for some interesting sex sometimes. Interesting both when it works and when it completely misses. I could totally tell this girl was into it.

About two minutes passed as we were making out on this girl's bed (I honestly don't remember her name), then out of nowhere, her body slowly went limp. Her eyes closed and gentle snores were being breathed. She passed out in my arms. I guess she wasn't into the pulling of the hair. Or maybe I just wasn't pulling hard enough to keep her awake. Dammit . . . Her body lay limp like a stuffed animal left on the side of a road.

I gently laid her body down from a sitting position so she can be more comfortable. What the hell should I do? I thought to myself. This chick was hot and I was horny as fuck. I sat there checking out her ass as she slept in the fetal position. I reached my hands out as if I was going to give both of her butt cheeks a massive grope. I stopped myself a couple inches from her sensual curves and my hands stood, empty. This chick is obviously passed out from the booze we had earlier, this is an easy opportunity to get some quick penetration and release and be gone before the pussy fully closes back up, I thought to myself. Hmmm, what a dilemma . . .

I sat there for a minute or two, looking around the room and contemplating what to do. The décor was like any other college dorm room. There was a small bed in which we laid in, a desk with a new laptop computer, papers and books scattered in an organized mess and clothes were dangling from the chair that stuck out from underneath. The closet was half open and I could see typical tops that a nice school girl would wear mixed in with some flamboyant garments that surely were used to pick up some frat boys. Not much else was in the room, other than the small nightstand beside the bed with a basic lamp that was probably bought at Target sitting on top.

My head was panning the room, looking for something to do to maybe try to wake this chick up. Maybe I could find something to drop on the floor to startle her awake, I thought. Or maybe turn on some lights and radio or something. My eyes swiveled and glanced at the laptop computer for a second time. A squint in one eye and a raised brow from the other would have shown anyone a light bulb flashed above my head. Dude, I can just walk right out of here with a brand new computer, I thought to myself. I looked back at the girl's beautiful ass. Or I could defile this girl as she sleeps, I thought. I again looked at the computer, then back at the girl's ass. The computer, then the girl's ass. This truly was a moral dilemma.

I hopped out of her bed, swiped the computer and took off out of her room. I hastily fled through the hallways and down the stairway that was the passage to my Firebird. There was no way I was going to rape this girl. I have morals. I have enough morality to know when it's wrong to sleep with someone. As for stealing, well, it's less harm than rape. The computer was probably just a present from the family, anyway. It took little convincing to reassure the tiny, disappointed angel that knelt above my left shoulder.

That time, I was unable to pull my famous quote that always led to a score, but another opportunity rose soon after the robbery incident.

After a night full of bar hopping and rejection, Ray and I spotted a group of four girls sitting outside of a pizza joint enjoying a few lingering slices left from a large pepperoni. As cocky and arrogant as I am, I still didn't have the balls to approach these four girls. Not only did they out-number us, but they were amazingly good looking. They were dressed in scantily clothes and they knew exactly what they wanted that night. None of this was a threat to Ray.

Ray walked over and sat at the same table as the girls and sparked up a quick conversation. I stood from afar and watched what went down. The unlucky night proceeding had my confidence in a sinkhole and I wanted to make sure it was a go before I actually went over to the group of females. I couldn't make out what was being said, but laughter was being exchanged between Ray and the four girls. So far, so good. I saw Ray entertaining all of them, but I could also tell he was focusing on one in particular.

Everything about this girl who was in Ray's sights was small. She was short and thin with a small, tight ass and small breasts. She had loads of makeup plastered on her face which made her look really pretty. With her tiny frame, she looked like a perfect match for Ray.

As soon as I knew everything was okay with these girls, I made my way over to the table to have a seat. A quick introduction and mentioning of our Army days had these girls melting through our fingertips. Our fake war recreations that took part in the mountains of Washington kept these chicks entertained for enough time before we all decided to head back to the home of one of the girls.

Fitting all of us into my sports car took some effort, but we all managed to squeeze in. Ray sat in one of the bucket seats in the back of the car with the girl he was talking up all night on his lap. Another girl sat on the center part between the two rear seats. With no cushioning at all, that poor girl must have been hurting the entire ride back. The two other girls occupied the remaining seats, with the one I was interested in up front with me.

Ray had his entire mouth wrapped around his girls face the entire ride back. Nothing would disturb these two. The other girls in the back were passed out from exhaustion. I tried to spark up a conversation to keep the one in front interested.

"So this is your mom's house were going to?" I began to ask her. "Have you thought about moving out on your own yet?"

"Look, I think there's something I need to tell you and your friend," she started to admit to me. "I'm not actually 19 years old like I told you earlier. I'm actually 17 years old."

God dammit, I said to myself. It started to sound like I won't be getting any action tonight. I can't sleep with an underage girl.

"You're 17?" I asked, as if somehow this question would make the previous revelation change. The problem was that the answer actually *did* change:

"Well," the girl began to say, "I'm not actually 17."

Jesus Christ. I knew exactly where this was going. I wondered just how low of an age she would go.

"I'm actually 15," she confessed.

"Wow, you're 15 years old?" I asked, shocked.

"Yeah, I'm a sophomore in high school," she told me. "Look, I'll totally understand if you guys wanna bail tonight. It's our fault you're in this mess. We led you on. So if you guys wanna take off, that's alright."

Even though this girl was only 15, she seemed like a pretty understanding person. She was pretty cool. This made me want to pound her even more, since she probably wouldn't rat us out. Haha, I'm just kidding.

"How old is your friend back there who's with my buddy?" I asked her.

"Dude, I'm sorry," she said to me, "she's only 13."

Holy fuck! The girl who is dry-humping Ray in the back seat of my car is only 13 years old! I exclaimed to myself in silence. We have a problem. There is absolutely no way we can go through with this. It's just wrong. It's not just wrong, it's disgusting.

Not much talk was had by us for the rest of the ride to the little girl's mom's house. Once there, we slipped out of the Firebird and made our way into the two-storey house. Once inside, everyone but me sat comfortably on a large couch and sofa.

I couldn't get myself to feel right about any part of this situation. Ray's mouth and lips still engulfed his girl's. The other three girls sat, relaxed and tired. Footsteps from the mother made their way down a stairway which was my and Ray's queue to step outside for a cigarette.

I pulled Ray's suction cups from the girl and dragged him outside while the mother started creating a small uproar inside.

"Dude, Ray, man," I said to him, "that chick you're with is only 13 years old, man."

He was still in a dream state from his brief love encounter. It took him a few moments to understand what I had just said.

"13?" he asked me for clarification. "She's fuckin' 13?!"

"Yeah, man," I answered back to him. "Let's get the fuck out of here."

"Fuck that, dude," he objected. "Let's just fuck 'em real quick and then get the fuck out of here."

"Dude, they know your real name," I began to explain to Ray. "They know you're in the Army and they have your name. If they ever decide to press charges, you're fucked. I won't be, but you will."

When I was out on the prowl, I would never use my real name because I knew it would one day come back to haunt me.

"Just let me stick my cock in her once," Ray stubbornly told me.

"What the fuck does that even mean?!" I started to get a tone with Ray and his persistence. "You're not sticking your cock in anything tonight, Ray. Let's get the hell outta here, man."

The 15 year old came outside to let us in on all of the ruckus that was happening on the inside of the house.

"Hey, you guys," she began to tell us. "My mom's being a bitch. Look, me and my friends will pay for a hotel for the six of us tonight."

"Fuck yeah!" Ray said to the girl with a gaping smile on his face as he approached her with his arm raised and hand sprawled out ready to give a high-five. "Let's take this shit somewhere else!"

"Look," I said to the girl. "You're cool for offering all this, but you know we can't go with you to a hotel. I appreciate the good time we had tonight."

"What?!" Ray said to me in disbelief. "Come on, yo, let's roll!"

I gave the girl a final tilt of my head and said to her, "You take it easy, alright?"

I grabbed Ray's arm and pulled him back to my car. He squirmed and cursed at me, still wanting to take the girls all the way. He was acting like a child who didn't get that candy bar at the checkout counter of a grocery store. This wasn't Ray's normal character, and I'm sure it was a reflection of the alcohol we had earlier. Few words were exchanged during the ride back to the barracks; we were both a bit tired anyway.

That night, I lay in bed unable to sleep with my mind preoccupied. I kept thinking to myself if that underage girl I talked to all night had slept with someone that was much too old for her. Surely I wasn't the first one that was successful in getting her back to her place for some action. And I know there are sick bastards out there who will fuck anything that gives them the chance. What happened that night with those girls must have happened before with an alternate ending from ours. I had a weird sense of concern for that group of girls. I had an uneasy feeling they didn't know exactly what they were doing and they would someday get hurt physically, if not, emotionally. I wished them all the best.

The next day, Ray put another worry I had to rest.

"Dude, thanks for draggin' me out of that situation last night," he told me. "I was too fucked up and horny to realize the mistake I would have made if I fucked that 13 year old."

I held out a closed fist to initiate a pounding of our friendship and said to Ray, "Don't fret, man. I got your back."

And with that, I confirmed Ray was human again.

Chapter Ten

I sat on a stool waiting for my two cards to be dealt to me as my girlfriend Sophia looked over my shoulder at the playing field. A short stack of casino chips was neatly piled directly in front of me, with my hands folded beyond them. My eyes jumped to the dealer's hands as he quickly began to lay out cards for each member sitting at the table. An eight of diamonds popped up near where my hands lay and my mind began to flip through a rolodex, trying to be ready with a betting solution by the time the next card was set.

The dealer's first card was set face down. Odds were against me to get closer to 21 than the dealer with my eight. A ten card was probably what the dealer had. I raised my right hand to nestle my heavy head. From my childhood, I always enjoyed gambling. Whether it was shooting dice in the school halls or playing poker at home with my father, a short adrenaline rush was reached every time those dice slid along the floor or every time I held five cards that shared the same suit. But when my money or poker chips begin to dwindle, the game gets to be frustrating and I want out faster than obscenities out of a Turrets sufferer.

The next card laid in front of me was the eight of clubs. Fucking great, I thought to myself. My grand total was now 16. A king of clubs flopped down from the dealer's hand onto the playing table next to him. My fate was sealed. If I was going to go down, I was going to go down hard, at least. The best thing to do in this situation is to stick with my 16 and lose as little money as possible. But it was time for me to leave this table and get on with something more important—drinking.

I grabbed two poker chips and pushed them next to the initial 20 dollar buy in bet. I was going to try my chances with splitting these eights up, hoping to get them to be accompanied by 10 spots. The dealer acknowledged my decision and flipped over two more cards for me, a nine of spades and a king of diamonds. I was looking at a hand that totaled 17 and a hand that equaled 18. I was just about ready to head to the nearby bar and start drinking. My feet reached for the ground.

The dealer showed his once faceless card. The jack of hearts laughed at me as my hand came down to hit the table. I let out a smirk, stood up and walked away with Sophia tailing me.

The cold, mid autumn air never breached the glass doors of the Indian Casino that Saturday night. My Army Company was hosting a party for a Staff Sergeant who was soon to be honorably discharged. The festivities were being held in a banquet room on the second floor of the casino, but I had quickly slipped away to do my own thing—which was to lose my money at the Blackjack tables. Now that that was over with, it was off to the bar.

Sophia and I walked over to a nearby glitzy bar top and ordered a Corona bottle and shot of Don Julio Silver tequila for each of us. We began to chat it up.

"Your friends are still coming down here to meet up with us?" I asked Sophia.

"Yeah," she answered me. "Janine and Candice are on their way. I want you to check out Candice's new tits; she just got them put in last week."

"Oh yeah?" I asked Sophia. "Has she seen a difference at work? Is she making more money now with them?"

"Fuck yeah," Sophia replied. "All the guys eat them shits up now."

Candice worked at a strip club just outside Fort Lewis—a perfect location. Thousands of lonely soldiers away from their lovers flocked to catch a glimpse of young, firm breasts rubbing against golden poles. Soldiers aren't as good of tippers as sailors, but the sheer number of soldiers that entered the joint every night more than made up for a lousy tip or two.

Our drinks arrived with haste as Sophia and I prepared for our shots of tequila. I licked my left hand, in the groove between the thumb and index finger, to make salt crystals cling onto me. Salt and lime makes tequila shots exponentially better. A quick, silent cheer with my girl and then the small glass was tipped, pouring the liquor into my mouth and down my throat. When all the content was emptied from the cup, I swung my free hand to my mouth to lick up the salt and then ultimately a lime slice was sucked on. Mmmm, top-grade stuff. This would be one of countless shots taken that night.

About 15 minutes and another shot of tequila later, Candice and Janine walked up and greeted me and Sophia.

"Hey, doll," Janine said to Sophia.

"Hi, hun," Sophia said back to Janine. "Grab a drink and kick back."

"Hiya, Frank," Candice greeted.

"What's up, girls," I said to the two of them.

Candice took a seat on one of my knees while Janine stood beside Sophia. Another round of drinks was ordered and the night had just begun.

There are many criminal offenses a person can have on their record which would prevent them from even being considered during the hiring process as a police officer. Besides the obvious murder, manslaughter or attempted murder charges, domestic violence is an offense that extinguishes the offender's chance to carry a weapon. A sheriff with no weapon on the streets of Los Angeles County is like a spider monkey walking into a gorilla's den in the forests of Congo. This night, I would fall prey to the domestic violence bug. It would also be a night branded as a tequila story, since I put all responsibility on the shoulders of the liquor.

I woke up to the sound of a metallic door being shut into a metallic frame. The clank rattled in my head for a few seconds and roused a mild headache. My eyes twitched open, cursing the bright lights shone upon them. I raised my torso from the floor and propped up my knees, making myself comfortable. I looked around and quickly noticed I wasn't alone in this holding cell. There were four others, two of them still sleeping, one pacing back and forth uttering some words that could not be heard, and the newest member settling into a bench.

First thing is first, I said to myself. I need to find out why I'm here. The night before is a complete blur to me. I don't remember a thing.

"What are you in here for?" I questioned toward the new guy.

He looked up and over at me and replied, "I got caught beatin' my wife."

I was surprised to hear he was married. The young man couldn't have been more than 25 years old. He was thin, but tall with a light brown mustache that matched the color of his mullet hair. Over his tank top, an old button-down, light blue collared shirt was worn, the type that would be seen with a name tag on it in a mechanic's garage. He wore brown worker pants and aging work boots. It looked as if he worked at a lumber yard.

"What are you doin' here?" he asked me.

I shook my head and said in a low voice, "I don't know."

I rose up and walked over to the door of the cage. The tequila from the night before took its toll on my body. I felt very weak and thirsty. A nauseating feeling twisted in my stomach at each breath taken, as if the air was dense with sulfur. My hands wrapped around the metal bars to stabilize myself.

A police officer leaned back on a chair that tilted near a desk just outside the cell, finishing up a crossword puzzle in the local newspaper.

"Hey," I called over to the cop. "I'm in the military, Army Infantry based out of Fort Lewis. You need to let my commanding officer know I'm in here."

"We already informed your unit about your circumstance," the police officer said back to me, not even taking an eye off his newspaper.

Good. So as long as I haven't done anything heinous enough, I should be out of here soon, I pondered to myself. As long as I didn't violate any federal laws, I'll get bailed out by someone from my unit.

With my hands still on the bars of the jail cell, I turned to the guy who paced back and forth and asked, "What's wrong with you? What are you in here for?"

He looked up from his downward stare, but not in my direction, and said to me, "Domestic violence."

Hmmm, two cases of domestic violence so far. Coincidence? I asked myself. It couldn't be. But how the hell could I be charged with domestic violence? Not a single one of my brain cells could ponder me as being a girlfriend beater. There has to be another explanation.

I cautiously made my way back to the corner of the room in which I sat before. I walked as if 40 years were added to my life the night before. My back was slightly hunched over and my legs bent and staggered. The 30 foot walk seemed like an endless journey. I felt like I needed to take a break after the first few steps. I looked around hoping to see a table with a representative handing out water and towels. But I only saw grey and cold. I desperately needed to rest, to regain my awareness.

My body lost all muscle tension as I reached the cave where I would spend the next 24 hours laying in. Without energy, nothing would disturb my sleep.

I awoke to lots of chatter amongst police officers that were shooting the shit just outside my holding cell. I finally felt rejuvenated. My body had recovered from a nasty fight with tequila. I was fresh with all of the rest I got and was ready to get the hell out of there. I was a bit confused, also, not seeing anyone from my unit come by to release me from this hole.

I walked up to my cage doors and asked the group of officers, "Hey, don't I get to make a phone call or something?"

One of the officers paused from his conversation, turned to me, then walked over and opened the gate to let me out. He recited my arraignment and confirmed my presumptions. I was there for domestic violence. Sophia will explain everything to me, I thought.

A call to my girlfriend and I was quickly out of that jail and in a car to freedom again.

"What the hell happened that night?" I asked Sophia.

"It was just a totally fucked up situation, Frank," she replied with a sympathetic face. "Those assholes at the casinos just wanted to fuck you."

She leaned forward, nestled her rear end more comfortably into her seat, raised her right hand from the steering wheel to gesture with and continued with her story:

"Alright, so we were all in the casino drinking these fuckin' cup-full shots of tequila. Of course, you got totally fucked up. I wanted you to check out Candice's new tits, so the both of you went into the girl's bathroom so you could have a look at them."

I smiled and raised my head confirming what Sophia told me. I at least remembered that part. She continued.

"I guess you were being all loud n' shit in there and someone must've told security or somethin'. When you came out, they were there waiting for you. I don't know what they said, but you guys started arguing with one another. You were gettin' all loud and creating a scene, so I went over to try to calm you down and settle the situation. The guy was saying shit like 'I'm gonna cut you off from drinkin' if you don't shut up' and shit like that. The both of us were getting mad, especially you. So you wanted to get the hell out of there."

Bewilderment was all over my face. I remembered none of this part.

"We went to the nearest exit, but it was like an emergency exit or somethin'. There was a security guy tryin' to stop us from exiting from there, but you know how stubborn you are. You were still tryin' to leave and you were pullin' me with you to get out. You kept tryin' to push your way through and you kept pullin' me. Then this big security guy comes and tackles you to the ground."

Ah, yes, I remember that, I said to myself.

"They cuffed you and waited for the cops to take you away. I guess those assholes couldn't pin anything else on you, so they gave you domestic violence. It's fucked up because they didn't even ask me anything."

"God dammit," was all I muttered out.

I sat back in my seat with my head leaned to watch the scenery drift by. At that moment, everything slowed to half its normal speed. That whole situation was going too fast and the falling browned leaves, the squirrel nibbling on its discovery, the birds scanning from above and the quiet sunlight shining down respectively went along the line of time. My brain was drowning from tumbling waves of thought. Consistency was void and only uncertainty, chaos remained. The absolute brilliance of a supernova explosion engulfed the pandemonium of a black hole. I again fell into feebleness.

It wasn't until about noon that I got back to my unit after a much needed shower at the barracks. My group was doing a routine gun qualification that Monday morning and afternoon, which had all members at the shooting range firing off rounds from our M16 assault rifles at targets 100 yards downfield.

I walked up to my squad leader, a sergeant, and reported in to him, "Alright, sarge, I'm all set to start my quals."

"Stiles," he replied to me, "where the fuck have you been? You're over five hours late."

A confused look came across my face and I answered him, "I was in jail. I've been in there since Saturday night."

A memory flashed in my mind of the previous day in jail. I remembered telling the guard that sat outside the cell to inform my unit and base about what had happened to me. I also remembered the jackass paying little attention to my plea. He didn't tell my commanding officer. What a dick.

"Well, that's the first any of us have heard about it," the sergeant told me. "You better go let the first sergeant know where the fuck you've been."

I wasn't quite sure how this was going to pan out. I was basically AWOL for a few hours. Soldiers and sailors take this quite seriously. During working hours, all personnel need to be accounted for at all times.

Infantry headquarters was where the first sergeant spent most of his time and it was also a short walk away. The building housed all the higher ranking Army personnel who usually have done enough time out in the field to spend the rest of their days in the comfort of a soft chair to deal with the mounds of paperwork the military spews out. I hated going in there to see all the khaki-uniformed soldiers walking about the cold hallways.

I have always had a problem dealing with authority, especially in the Army. The system was to blame, mostly, because we were taught from day one to always obey and respect those who were ranked higher than you. The problem lay with soldiers who slither their way to a respectable rank, despite how incompetent they are. The snakes get there only because they have served for a long time and basically 'had' to get promoted. These soldiers who shared an IQ with a garbage can were littered throughout the ranks of the military and I found it extremely difficult to pretend to show any form of respect for these useless soldiers. But this isn't just limited to the armed forces; it's found in most jobs.

I quickly walked through the maze of corridors to my first sergeant's office, trying to avoid any eye contact with others. I reached the small office of my overseer, gave a two-tap knock on the open door and walked inside to have a seat.

"Ah, Stiles," my first sergeant began to tell me, "it's so nice of you to fuckin' show up. Where the hell have you been?"

"Yes, first sergeant, I'm sorry," I reported. "I have been in jail since Saturday night."

I was hoping that giving him the notice of me spending more than a day locked up would make him sympathize.

"Jail?" he questioned. "Why were we not informed? What were you in for?"

"Yes," I explained. "I told the cops to tell my unit where I was and what happened, but they obviously didn't. They got me with a domestic violence charge."

A burst of laughter from my first sergeant filled the room. I guess that tickled his fancy.

His laughter diminished and then he said to me, "Ah, domestic violence! Happens to all of us! She probably deserved it, anyways."

A smile came over my face.

"Just take care of it on the civilian side and we'll leave you alone over here," he said. "We won't write you up or anything, just carry on back to work as usual. Now get the hell outta here, soldier."

I went back to my unit to give them a half-day's work then searched for a lawyer after closing time.

I met up in the office of my lawyer later that week. I honestly admit I chose that guy solely based on his name: Mickey Lucky. The office was very New Age—not like the typical lawyer office one envisions. There weren't bookshelves full of fat, monotone literature that would only interest an academic. Credentials weren't plastered all over the walls like a botched wallpaper job. Not even the dark, scholarly color scheme of the Hollywood-invented lawyer's den was apparent. It was a very simple room with little inside. The walls were painted—or I should say, left—white, with a large desk in the middle of the room. A flat screen monitor was the only visible sign of a computer. It sat on the corner of the desk, with a lava lamp behind it for a client to gaze upon. A corner table was toward the back of the room, with a small Bose radio on it. A small shelf with thick binders was in the far right corner of the room, probably filled with law jargon.

Mickey, himself, didn't seem like the normal lawyer. He wore a suit, yes, but he definitely did not belong in one. He didn't even know how to choose a proper one. The jacket was slightly too large, and the trousers were slightly too short. Both had extremely feint white pinstripes amongst a deep blue surface. Lucky had long hair, but not too long where it touched his shoulders. It wasn't combed, just tossed, like a surfer does during low tide. His skin was tanned to a sparkling light brown hue, odd for a native of Washington State. He was definitely a person you could call a drinking buddy.

I sat in a chair opposite the desk from where Lucky was. He had been briefed about my situation before I arrived and wasted little time.

"I'm going to tell you right away," he began to explain, "domestic violence is huge out here in the northwest and every case seems to get hammered by the judge. You're probably going to get this on your record, and it's a serious charge. You'll be branded with this and you won't be able to carry a weapon ever again, amongst other ailments."

This wasn't sounding good at all. No gun, no future as a police officer. I was hoping there was some sort of silver lining embedded in all this madness.

"I'm only speaking the truth about the matter," Lucky continued. "There is no silver lining in this at all. And it gets worse: I've read the details about your court hearing. The judge that will be on the stand has a 'thing' for domestic violence."

This keeps getting better and better, I thought to myself in an exaggerated fashion. I'm surely going to get screwed with this.

"Do you think I'll get busted with this even though my girlfriend says I didn't do anything to her?" I asked Mickey.

"Again, this judge really doesn't care about how innocent you may seem," he replied. "She's going to try to get you just for the nature of the situation."

"Well, just do your best to help me out," I said in a defeated voice.

"That, I will do, my friend," Lucky tried to reassure me.

Not much else was discussed at that meeting with the lawyer. He knew already what was going down and how to go about in trying to prevent the charge from appearing on my record. I was sure he dealt with this kind of thing before and knew the ins and outs about it.

The day of the trial had arrived. It was set in the evening, so I only had to skip out slightly early from work to make it on time to court.

Sophia and I walked into the courtroom and up to the long table where my lawyer Mickey was already sitting. He had a big grin on his face as I pulled up a chair and sat down.

"You're in luck, Stiles," Lucky said to me. "The scheduled judge isn't here to deliver your trial. We got a replacement."

"Ah, yes," I said in relief, "finally some good news. Let's hope the one that shows up is cool."

"Yeah, but don't get too excited," he brought me back to reality. "We still got a female judge over us. Let's see if she's a feminist."

The few members in the courtroom were ordered to stand to show respect as the judge made her way in the room and to her post. She was a stern-looking woman, one that took care of business, it seemed. She had a face that looked very professional and well-educated. She had bushy eyebrows that went along with her graying short hair. Her tall, wiry frame was easily seen behind the large podium with her perfect posture. A hint of facial blush, mascara and lipstick was artistically drawn on her visage. The room sat when the order was given.

"Here we have the case of a Mr. Frank Stiles versus the State of Washington," she said with a bold voice. "Prosecutor, let's try to get this done today. What do you have for me?"

"Absolutely, your honor," the legal representative responded. "The defendant is accused of domestic violence that occurred on the night of the 30th of November of this year at the Wudoku Indian casino."

"Your honor," the prosecutor continued, "after speaking with the defendant's lawyer and after careful review of the incident via the casino's cameras, I declare that no law was broken by the defendant. The victim was free from harm as seen on the cameras."

The dark clouds that hovered above me were beginning to clear up. Could there finally be a trickle of sunshine in my future? I hoped for the best, but the decision wasn't up to the prosecution. My fate lay in the hands of the judge.

"The state recommends the domestic charge be deferred for one year with conditions for the defendant. These conditions are listed on the document before you," the prosecutor finished his statement.

The judge read the statement and conditions in front of her. I could see her head going from side to side as she quickly read the file. Her eyes squinted a bit and she seemed very hesitant. I could tell she didn't want to agree with the state.

She lifted up her head toward Sophia and asked, "Sweetheart, did he hurt you in any way at all?"

Sweetheart? I questioned to myself. This bitch hates men.

"No, ma'am," Sophia told the judge. "Frank didn't harm me at all; he was just helping me out of the building."

The robed judge leaned forward and put her elbows upon the stand. She respectively interlocked the fingers of both her hands and gave out a sigh. She did nothing to mask her hesitation.

"With that, I hereby accept the prosecution's verdict as my own," the judge began to lay down the conditions. "Frank Stiles, the charge of domestic violence will be deferred for one year. This time will be noted as your probation time. If I see you in court within this year of probation for any reason, you will be fully charged with domestic violence thereafter. A mandatory domestic violence and anger management class will be completed by the defendant during this year of probation. This is my verdict. This case is now adjourned."

With the slam of a gavel, I was off the hook. I never should have been on the hook in the first place. I never committed any crime. I never hit or abused my girlfriend. I would never do such an act, even with the devil himself—tequila—lurking inside of me.

"You lucky son of a bitch," Lucky whispered to me as he stretched out his hand to congratulate me.

I replied with an almost sinister smile and shook his hand. Little did I know, I would need his assistance nine days later.

Chapter Eleven

"The police report says that you told the arresting cop you had drunk 10 beers that night after he asked you how much you had to drink," my lawyer Mickey Lucky told me during my second meeting with him at his office. He had a look of confusion under a growing smile. "I mean, don't people usually say something like 'Sorry officer, I had one or two beers a couple of hours ago'?"

"Man, I was drunk," I replied to Lucky. "I didn't know what to say. He didn't like me, anyway, so it didn't matter what I said."

"And what makes you think he didn't like you?" my lawyer asked.

"The guy was an ex-Military Police," I began to explain. "I told him that I was in the Army Infantry hoping that he would go easy on me. He said he was an MP. MP's hate infantrymen. They always gotta bust us."

Mickey flipped through his notes, skimming the material.

"Let's see," he paused. "The report says you blew a .18 on the breathalyzer and you failed a field sobriety test."

I didn't see any problem so far. It surely was because the cop hated infantrymen.

"The cop goes on to say that you hit the curb as you pulled into the gas station where the arrest was made and you stumbled as you got out of your car."

Mickey continued, "Now, the report says that he initially pulled you over because your headlights weren't on. But you have all these other red flags going up, so I can't really find a way to dismiss the DUI. And I'm sure I don't have to remind you that you're on probation with this other domestic violence thing. This will surely pop flares and trigger the domestic violence charge."

Mickey Lucky's smile and feint laughs quickly drifted away and a contemplative look crept onto his face. He raised his arm to his face and placed the cusp of his hand under his freshly shaven chin. His eyebrows tightened and silence was in the air. Pages were flipping inside of Lucky's mind.

After a drawn out stillness, Mickey said to me, "Okay, look. There's not much that we can do. So, we're just going to go to court, act like normal, and see if maybe—just by luck—they don't see the prior domestic violence charge."

"You're probably gonna get the DUI charge, there's not much I can do about that," Mickey kept explaining. "Let's just cross our fingers about the domestic violence yellow flag not being tossed into the field."

"You're the expert," I told my lawyer. "And I realize I'm not giving you much to work with."

It was New Year's Eve, just before 2003. I was at a bar in downtown Seattle with my girlfriend Sophia. The night was going well, the holiday season kept laughs and smiles floating in all directions. Tequila shots had a short life span that night.

Festivities were high, along with morale and happiness.

The new year hadn't even begun when I yelled out to Sophia, "Fuck you! Why are you getting mad about the chicks that I've fucked in the past?"

"Frank," Sophia began her rebuttal, "don't bring that shit up out of nowhere. We were talking about my friends and then all the sudden you start saying shit about some black chick you've fucked in the past."

"I didn't bring that shit up, you made me say that shit," was all I could blurt out.

"Just shut the fuck up, Frank," Sophia tried to end the argument.

"Fuck you and fuck this," I stood up out of my chair. "I'm gettin' the fuck outta here."

"What the fuck, Frank?" Sophia said with concern. "You can't leave. You're too fucked up to drive home. I'll take you back."

"Fuck that," I said to her as I made my way out of the small bar. "You're staying here. Stay the hell outta my way."

Sophia's concern stayed in the bar with her. I walked reasonably straight as I took out my keys and unlocked the door to my dusty Firebird. I took a seat, slammed the door shut, threw the car into reverse and quickly pushed the accelerator down. I backed into a parked car then nonchalantly sped away onto the highway, reaching a speed of about 100 miles an hour in a matter of seconds. And in a matter of seconds after reaching top speed, a flicker of red and white lights were visible in my rearview mirror. I had a split second to make a decision. A flashback rolled in my mind of something that happened to me about a year ago.

I was with my buddy Dirty Duncan in my car driving home from a friend's house in the backwoods of Washington. We were both drunk from lots of beers, lost in the unlit wilderness and my car was running out of fuel. I was doing about 120 miles per hour. Why? Well, because in that car, I could. There was nothing in sight. No buildings, no gas stations, no signs of civilization. We were the only car on the road for about 10 minutes when we finally saw another car quickly approaching us in the opposite direction. We zoomed right past one another, in opposite lanes, in the blink of an eye. Naturally, I looked in the rear view mirror. The car we had just passed turned out to be a police officer's. It made a difficult u-turn and flipped on the light bar, signaling me to pull over to the side of the road. I turned my head towards Duncan. Speaking with only my eyes, I told him, "Hold on tight, I'm floorin' it."

I pressed the accelerator even further towards to chassis of the car. The needle on the speedometer was inching toward the 150 mark. Our bodies were being pushed by the g-force and it seemed as if the trees marked by the peripherals of my headlights were in a different parallel universe. We were in a bubbled vessel going against all natural things.

The lights that shone in my rear view got smaller and smaller, more and more feint. I was hoping not to run into a sharp turn in the road the entire getaway. We were going much too fast to safely bank a right or left. Even in my low-profile sports car, any tight turn would probably cause us to overturn countless times like an out-of-control roller coaster you find at an amusement park.

Our high speed time traveling came to an end after what seemed to be about two minutes when I saw a low, reddish-orange light coming down from a lone light pole just outside of a church. At the sight of that, I flipped off my car lights and quickly reduced my speed to make a sharp turn into the church parking lot. I drove towards the back of the church, far away from the highway, and parked where no light could reach. Duncan and I crouched a bit in our seats, thinking the police officer may see the one-ton vehicle but might possibly overlook the two people sitting inside. We were playing peek-a-boo with a grown man.

Neither of us said a word to one another as we awaited a blurred black and white vehicle to pass our line of sight. We were both drunk, underage, speeding past a misdemeanor's limit and now we were evading arrest. Surely, if caught, the police could tack on other charges, like reckless driving and public endangerment.

It seemed as if decades had passed, and then we finally saw the cop's vehicle fly by. He must have been in a hurry. Duncan and I stood in silence and with little movement for about another 25 minutes. We didn't want to take any more chances with this.

I finally got the courage to creep my car up to the driveway of the church, where an angel must have been sent down to look out for our illegal acts. Once at the driveway and after a quick look at the emptiness of the road, I sped off to continue my search for a gas station. This time, we kept a reasonable speed.

Just as my car was about to run out of its last reserve of fuel, a gas station appeared in the distance. I conspicuously and calmly pulled alongside a fuel pump and began to fill up the tank as if nothing had happened a few minutes prior. As the car was getting filled up, I made my way inside the mini mart to relieve myself of the useless parts of the beer I had drunk earlier that night. Before returning to my car, I grabbed a bottle of Pepsi to drink on the way home.

I pulled the nozzle out of the gas tank after the final drops were deposited, made sure everything was in order, and began the final journey home.

As I pulled out of the gas station, I could still smell gasoline. It was very pungent, and must have been coming from inside of the car. I lifted my arms and looked down at myself to see if any fuel had spilled onto my clothing. I smelled my hands to check for the same, but nothing was apparent. Then, I looked over at Duncan. He had an ominous grin on his face and he couldn't hold in the laughter.

"What the hell is so funny?" I asked Dirty.

Duncan didn't say a word, he just continued to laugh. By that time, we were within the city limits and there were many cars with us on the highway.

Dirty rolled the passenger side window completely down.

"Dude, what the fuck are you doing?" I yelled toward him. "It's cold!"

He reached down to where his feet were and pulled up a circular object. It seemed like it weighed a considerable amount, given its relatively small size. He laid the object on his lap and took a quick look out of the window.

"What the hell is that?" I asked him, not expecting a response since none of my other pleas were attended to.

But he didn't have to answer me. I knew what it was. It was what was causing the stench of gasoline. It didn't belong there in my car; it belonged to the gas station.

Gas stations keep their main supplies underground, in large tanks that can hold up to 35,000 gallons of fuel, depending on how much business it gets. Truck tankers restock the massive containers when requested, through a pipeline that runs to the surface. This pipeline is covered by a thick metal cover, roughly the diameter of a basketball. This cover was commandeered by Dirty.

Duncan gave another quick look out of the window then gave the metal cover a strong toss out of my car and onto the asphalt of the highway.

"Holy fuck!" I yelled out as I leaned my head and sight towards his window to catch a glimpse of where the top had landed.

Missing the loud merging of metal and blacktop, I stood back in my seat and gave a stare into my rear view mirror. It was like the 4th of July on Venice Beach with thick sparks spraying every which way. It looked like a small explosion had just detonated on the highway with all the light emitted. I couldn't look for very long; I didn't want to witness a car accident caused by this skipping foreign object. What I don't see doesn't happen.

All of this flashed in my mind in a millisecond. I succumbed to the decision to ironically pull over into a gas station.

I sat in my car and just had an angry blank stare off into nowhere. The police officer stepped out of his vehicle and approached my door. My window was already rolled down for the two of us to discuss my situation more easily.

"You know why I pulled you over?" he said in a half rhetorical fashion.

"Please enlighten me," I replied back to him.

He gave a wince at me, and at that time I knew he had smelled all the booze on my breath.

"You have a busted taillight," he said to me. "Not to mention the case of beer you're keeping in your mouth."

"Look, officer," I began to plead. "I'm in the Army Infantry. Can you cut me some slack this time and give me a warning?"

"You're in the infantry?" he repeated. "I'm an ex-MP. I used to get sick of busting you arrogant mother fuckers. You assholes think you're the shit."

He took a step back and proceeded to say, "I'm going to have to ask you to step out of your vehicle for a field sobriety test."

I got out of my car. As far as I remember, I didn't stumble. But who am I to say what exactly happened; I was drunk. The officer led me to a straight white line painted on the pavement to indicate a parking space.

"See this line here," he told me, pointing with the toe of his boot. "I want you to try to follow this line as accurately as you possibly can."

I began to walk the line. My arms came up, outstretched to gain more stability. It didn't help much. I couldn't keep my balance on the tightrope. My feet were dancing all around the line, making little contact with the target. At one point, I thought of myself as a tap dancer performing his last gig before retirement.

The police officer grabbed my left arm to keep me from falling. "Okay," he said, "I think I have seen enough here. Step over to the rear of your vehicle."

He pulled out a small device from a pouch on his duty belt. It was a breathalyzer. I'm sure this wasn't normal to have with the person, but given the New Year's Eve circumstances, that little machine would send many people to jail that night.

He reloaded the breathalyzer with a new, clean mouthpiece and forcefully placed it into my mouth.

"I want you to give a very hard blow into this," he said, referring to the breathalyzer.

I followed his instructions to avoid any hassles. I was feeling a bit fatigued from the argument earlier with Sophia. My bladder also felt as if it were about to explode. I needed to urinate more than ever and getting this charade over with as quickly as possible would prevent any emergency room visits.

The police officer popped the tester out of my mouth and turned me around. He began to administer handcuffs. I guess he wanted to tie down my stabilizers.

"Sir, you're under arrest," he began to announce. "You failed my field sobriety test and blew a point one eight on the breathalyzer. You are under arrest for driving under the influence of alcohol."

He led me to the back of his squad car and gently placed me into the bucket seat. Every movement made a small trickle of piss come out of me. I had to release this beast quick before the Bellagio water special was to come pouring out.

We made a u-turn in the gas station parking lot and drove away in the direction in which we came from. In the car, I could hear the radio transmitter spewing off chatter from many different sources. The cop held the speaker, which acted as both transmitter and receiver, up to his right ear. More ranting occurred.

"10-4, I will drop off the suspect at my current location of Sycamore and 18th," the ex-MP relied to one of the voices that came from the speaker. "I will need a taxi cab to recover the arrested to escort him to safety."

"Roger that," I heard from the transmitter. "A taxi is on the way."

"Alright, check this out," the police said to me. "The jail is overrun with suspects tonight. So, we're going to cite and release you. Your court date and details are listed on the citation. A cab has been called to pick you up. It will drive you back to your home. Do you understand?"

"Yeah, yeah," I responded, still feeling rushed by the tidal wave that lurked in my urinary tract.

"I'm on a mission," the police officer said to me. "Let's get you the hell outta here so I can take care of something else."

With that, the cop hopped out of his car and let me out of the back seat. In a swift motion, he unlocked the handcuffs and I was free. Free to piss.

"Stay here until the cab arrives," the officer ordered.

As he made his way into the squad car, my jeans were already unzipping. The button above the fly of my pants was unpinned when the cop car started. And with the police officer still in sight, my penis flopped out and erupted with a spectacle that belonged at a water park. It was better than sex. The gushing flow of relief towered high above any orgasm in my past. I stood with my 'oh' face for nearly an entire minute. It was pure satisfaction. The semi-clear liquid flowed down and created an indention in the mud, where it hit the ground. A small, frothy lake was forming beneath me. The heat and stench pierced through my nostrils and reminded me of unattended public restrooms in the middle of a hot summer day. I took tiny steps back and to the side, to avoid sinking into this newly formed resort for ants. I let out an amazing sigh of relief, did a quick shake, and then clothed myself back up again.

Shorty after, my cab drove up and the driver rolled down the window to ask, "You call for a cab?"

Without answering, I jumped into the back seat, sat forward and pointed in the direction of the gas station that held custody of my beautiful car.

I ordered to the cab driver, "Take me three blocks that way."

It wasn't three minutes later I was back on the highway doing 120 miles per hour, still drunk. If I was to get pulled over again, I wouldn't hesitate to make another run for it.

My doomsday had arrived. It was late in the afternoon and I didn't have time to go back to my barracks to change out of my camouflage work outfit after spending the day out in the field. In a rush to not make a bad impression of tardiness, I weaved in and out of traffic to get to the courtroom by the 1500 hour deadline to calmly discuss the repercussions of my recent DUI charge.

After hastily and terribly parking in the slanted slots just outside of the courthouse, I ran to the appropriate hearing where my lawyer Mickey Lucky was waiting.

"Good, you made it on time," he said to me in relief.

Out of breath, I said back to him, "Yep, wouldn't miss this for the world."

"Cross your fingers, mother fucker," Lucky sarcastically mentioned to me. "We're going to need divine intervention for us to pull this off the way we want."

The routine court check was underway and soon enough, the session commenced. This time, the judge who overlooked the case was male. He had a firm demeanor in every one of his actions, much like the female who presided over my domestic violence case.

"Prosecutor, what do you have for me?" the judge delegated.

"Your honor, we have the State of Washington versus Frank Stiles. The defendant is accused of driving under the influence of alcohol on the night of December 31st, 2002," the prosecutor announced to the courtroom and judge.

"How do you plea, sergeant?" the judge asked me.

"I'm guilty, your honor," I admitted.

"Then that's that," the judge told everyone. "Sergeant Stiles, you are to report back to this courtroom in four months for sentencing purposes."

It was time for mine and Lucky's curve ball. We had an idea.

"Your honor, if I may intervene," Mickey gallantly stated. "My client is due for deployment into Iraq in April of this year for an undetermined amount of time. We ask the court if we may postpone the sentencing until he returns safely home."

"Could you please present to the court documents formally stating the defendant's departure," the prosecutor countered.

"We apologize," Mickey stayed on his ground, "but Mr. Stiles had this news shed upon him very recently and we are unable to attain these documents in such a short time."

The prosecutor shook his head toward Mickey then turned to the judge. "Your honor, the court needs a proper notice of his April departure in writing in order to comply with the request," he said.

The judge shook his head toward the prosecutor then turned to me. "Son, when will you deploy to Iraq?" he asked me.

"Sir, the date for departure is the 6th of April," I tried to sound as respectful as possible.

Focus was set back to the prosecutor. The judge gave a harsh look at the prosecutor and boldly said, "If a sergeant of the United States Army tells me he is going to get deployed, then he is going to get deployed."

He then spoke to Mickey and I, "Come back in June, 14 months after your departure. We will take care of it then, soldier."

The judge stood and walked down from the podium. Mickey and I kept straight faces. We hid our joy very well. As soon as the robed man was out of the room, we briskly walked out of the back door.

Once in the hallway we turned to one another and gave an exaggerated sigh of relief. Mine was coupled with a contorted back bend.

"Jesus Christ, Stiles," Mickey said to me with a grimace, "you are the luckiest son of a bitch I have ever seen."

"Holy shit," I hollered, "you got that right!"

"How the hell did the previous charge held against you not pop up on their radars?" he asked, not expecting a response.

"You're my lucky charm, Lucky," I told him. "You need to come hit the casinos with me so we can get rich."

"Alright man, you think you can stay out of trouble for at least a few days? I don't want to get a phone call from you next week of you telling me you got caught fuckin' a goat or some stupid shit like that," Lucky jokingly said.

"Sheep are the way to go," I smartly replied. "They don't fight it."

I stuck out my hand and gave Mickey Lucky a firm handshake to show him my sincere gratitude. He didn't actually do much to help me with the cases; it was more of a properly set of dealt cards. But at that moment, I couldn't help but think he was why I was now on two separate probations and my domestic violence charge would be expunged by the time sentencing for the DUI was to go down. I could see that he understood my voiceless appreciation as I stared into his eyes. My left eye gave a soft movement, as if I was about to wink, then I released the grip I had on his hand and went my separate way.

Chapter Twelve

Police officers get to meet all sorts of interesting people while on the job. The more an officer knows about what the human mind is capable of doing and thinking, the better decisions he can make that may one day safe a life. No two minds think alike. Everyone has the ability to create any type of reality for oneself. These realities can be a routine life with a set nine to five job in downtown with a two storey, three bedrooms, two point five baths house in the suburbs. This reality can come equipped with a marriage to a beautiful woman who bore two point three children. That point three of a child could be the family dog, cat, houseplant or whatever.

On the other hand, one of these realities could be filled with distortion. Everything seen in the eyes of this alternate creator could have a demise manifested and played out through each clicking synapse. One of these images may be of a jogger being pushed into the path of a relentless city bus by one of these sick people. It could be of a mallet smashing the side window of an SUV and cracking the skull of an eight year old passenger. Every human mind is different, in sickness and health. The more exposure to the variations of human thought, the more understanding of capability.

After about a year in Washington, I had earned lots of vacation days and was ready to blow three week's worth to spend some time with some friends back in California. The weekend before my leave, I wanted to get the celebration started earlier than planned. I grabbed my wingman Ray, popped a couple ecstasy pills and then we were on our way to the rave scene at Keen.

It didn't take long for the pills to kick into effect. My mind was swimming and I couldn't hold on to a solid thought. The increased dose was surely the reason. At this stage, I was used to taking two capsules of ecstasy before getting the party started. This time around, I threw down double that amount. I remembered everything that was happening, whether I wanted to or not.

Driving along the main highway to get to Keen, my car began to putter like a sick dog. I made sure the accelerator was pressed down, but didn't understand what the hell was going on. It was as if the car would accelerate for a second, then need to rest for two or three seconds before starting the pattern up again. I was driving like a teenager who first stepped foot into a car.

"Dude, what the fuck is up with this thing?" I half-rhetorically asked toward Ray. "I'm pushing down the gas, but it won't go."

Ray looked over to the display panel beyond the steering wheel. "You dumbass," he said to me. "You're out of gas."

"Ah, shit," I uttered.

With the car still directly in the middle of the road, I pressed the brake to come to a complete stop. Once idle, I put the car in park and got out.

"What the hell are you doing?" Ray yelled at me.

"Let's walk to that gas station up there," I pointed about a half-mile up the road.

"What the fuck?" Ray scolded again with a high voice. "You can't just leave this thing in the middle of the street. Help me move it off the street."

"Oh, shit," I said back to him in epiphany. "I guess you're right."

I walked back to the driver's side door, opened it, and reached in to put the car into neutral gear so we could easily push it. The shifter wouldn't budge. I forcefully wiggled it back and forth to get only a slight response, with it staying in the 'P' setting.

"Dude, put the keys in the ignition first," Ray said. This time I could hear his voice easing with patience. He probably realized I would be acting like a three year old for a little while, so it would be best to keep his cool.

With some guidance, the car was onto the shoulder of the road. A five-minute walk proceeded.

We got to the gas station and went directly into the mini-mart attached. I made my way to the refrigerated items toward the back of the store while Ray had a look at the snack aisle. Quickly, I snatched up two one-gallon jugs of 2% milk. 2% is what I was raised with and I wouldn't dare touch the watery non-fat stuff.

I made my way to the check-out counter to stand in line. Ray came up from behind me.

"Dude, what are you doing?" he asked me with a confused look on his face.

"What does it look like I'm doing?" I smartly said to him. "I'm buying gas for the car."

"Wow, man," Ray said in disbelief. "Dude, put that away, I'll take care of it."

I stood aside to let Ray take care of gassing up the jugs he just bought. He even demanded to carry them, still unsure of my mental well-being.

On the way back to the car, we heard a voice calling from a cemetery that stood next to the gas station. "You guys need any help?" it asked.

Both Ray and I looked to our left, past the chain-linked fence and saw a young man dressed in coveralls tending to a recently covered grave. It was a bit eerie seeing him beneath the only light emitted from the only light pole on that street.

"Nah, we got it under control," Ray said to him.

"Cool," the guy acknowledged. "Where you headed?"

"We're goin' to check out what's crackin' at Keen," Ray answered.

"Aight," the man said with an upward nod. "You guys care if I come with? We can all do a couple bong hits before . . ."

I looked over at Ray and said to him in a low voice, "Dude, let's pick this guy up. I haven't smoked weed in forever."

Ray looked over to the guy and said, "Alright. Where you got it at?"

"Throw that gas can over the fence and come on over," he told us. "My pad's just right over here."

I found it a bit strange that this guy lived on a cemetery, but quickly got over it, given my condition at that time. Scaling the fence was no problem, though.

We got to this guy's house, which seemed to be in the middle of the cemetery. I didn't even want to label it as a house. It was more like a shack. I could have gone down to the local hardware store to pick up a shed in the storage department and have an equivalent shelter.

Inside, there was only an old, ragged couch, a creaky wooden coffee table, and a small television sitting on top of a stack of old magazines. Clothes were thrown off into a corner of the shack.

"Pop a squat on the couch there," he told Ray and me. "The name's Jackson."

"Ray," Ray said to Jackson, pointing at himself with his thumb and fist clenched. "This guy's Frank."

"Let me get this thing fixed up for you," Jackson said pulling a massive bong out of thin air like a magician would do. "You guys just kick back."

Ray and I made ourselves comfortable on the stained couch. We both kept looking around the small room, but didn't say much. The only thing going through my mind at that time was 'What type of person could live in such a place like this?'. My curiosity got the best of me and needed to be quenched.

"So what's with the whole cemetery gig?" I asked Jackson.

"Man, I've been living on the streets since I was 14," he answered me. "Been livin' with all different kinds of people and doin' all kinds of different jobs to try to stay alive."

Yeah, he seemed like the typical case of 'child kicked out of the home never to return'. Even though I had never met the parents of this guy, I probably wouldn't blame them on their decision. This Jackson fellow had delinquent written all over his face. Soon after his exile, he most likely began a life of petty crimes, which probably included but not limited to burglary, possession of illegal substances, underage drinking and grand theft auto. But who am I to judge? Those were the cards this man was dealt.

"There we are," said Jackson. "We're all set. You guys puff on this for a minute while I hit these lines. Speak up if you want in."

The lines he was referring to were lines of methamphetamine. I didn't want to push myself too far over the edge, so I didn't partake. Ecstasy and weed was plenty for me on that night.

Ray started with a deep hit from the bong. He let the herb sink into his lungs for a handsome amount of time before exhaling. A short pause, then another deep hit—but not as profound as the first. With the smoke still inside of him, Ray nudged the bong toward my direction, signaling it was my turn.

My lungs felt like virgins all over again. It had been so long since they had touched the scent of cannabis. It only took two good hits for me to be high as a corrupted angel. And with that, I was practically incapacitated. I felt like I couldn't rise up from the sofa. My body sank deep into the cushion and everything I looked at was blurred. All my senses slowed to quarter speed, which explained the echoing I heard. It felt great.

The bong had made its way over to Jackson. It was no stranger to him. He nestled the bowl in between his legs, gave it a light and he soon was in heaven with the rest of us.

"Alright, y'all," he said to us. "We can't let this high go to waste. Let's get the hell outta here and hit up the rave."

I nodded and the next thing I knew I was being helped out of the shed by Ray. My legs were floating six feet above the grass as we walked to my car just outside the cemetery. Apparently time didn't slow for everything else around me—I quickly found myself in the driver's seat of my car.

I inserted the key into the ignition, gave it a turn and immediately accelerated into the guard rail on the opposite side from which I was supposed to be going. Obviously, I was in no condition to drive.

"Fuck man, I can't drive," I admitted. "I'm too fucked up right now."

"Dude, I can't either," Ray said to me and Jackson.

"No worries, fellas," the new guy said to us. "I got it under control. I'm cool to drive."

I had never let anyone else drive my car before that night. Under no circumstance before did foreign hands touch the steering wheel to my precious Firebird. It was a sacred bond the car and I shared. She took care of me. I would never let another person be a mistress of my ride—until that day. Good choice, too—this guy who was about to adulterate my car just finish smoking weed and doing lines of meth. Well, I guess it was a good choice since we got to Keen safely.

At the rave, I remember sitting along one of the walls the entire night, feeling every pound of bass from the massive speakers. The combination of weed and ecstasy had me in a euphoria that matched the feeling I had when I first tried either drug. My head energetically nodded to every beat, but my eyes remained shut with a large grin across my face.

Moments like this are rare in life. A simple state of mind and occasion can bring an amazing happiness unique to an individual. When a person looks back at their lives to the times when they felt the most joy it is usually a period of complete relaxation brought by simplicity.

I recall one other episode of my life when I shared a similar feeling. It was a time when I lived in the entertainment capital of the world—Las Vegas. I look back at the time frame when I spent days doing nothing in my apartment other than snorting lines of cocaine while playing my favorite video game online against what sounded like mostly children. I would hear young voices through my headset cursing up a storm toward my character as he owned all other players.

Every person can relate to this in their own personal way. Try to recall an era in your past when you didn't have to worry about what happened at work; when your children were taken care of by another entity; when your income or debt weren't a concern; when all homework was completed and tests were all studied for; when you didn't have a care in the world other than the one that dealt with that particular thing you do to pass the time. This special thing could be—but doesn't always have to be—unique to you and only you. It can be playing the online gaming sensation World of Warcraft; it can be jamming out on your electric guitar or drum set; it can be watching your favorite cartoon sitcom character setting up one more extravagant flashback of his; it can be baking that special banana nut bread that only you can make; or it can be reading how your favorite author's plot gets dissected. Thinking back to the combination of this time of carelessness and playing out your unique activity will make your eyes close and pinch as tranquility and nostalgia fill your being. These times of simplicity are what humans strive to attain. I was there.

After the weed wore off, the night got old fairly quick. I was ready to get out of there not long past midnight. I stood and wandered about for a few minutes to track down my colleagues. Accidentally, I stumbled upon Jackson.

"Hey dude," I began to tell him. "We're gonna get outta here. I'm losin' my buzz."

"You wanna keep the party goin' at my buddy's place?" Jackson asked me as he pointed to his friend who stood next to him. "He's got weed and drink at his pad."

I gave Jackson's friend an examination with my eyes. He was a strange looking guy, not only in personality, but in physical features. Firstly, his eyes were set slightly too far apart from one another, which made it seem like they never focused on the same object at a particular given time. What made it worse was his eyes' apparent lack of dryness. This guy didn't blink very much, and when he did, it was a hell of a blink. His eyelids and eyelashes were like a Venus flytrap chomping down on a pupil of a fly. They would stay shut for the better portion of a second.

"Yeah, sure, man," I agreed to Jackson's offer. "What's this guy's name?"

"His name's Emry," Jackson responded. "He doesn't talk much, either."

Emry's shoulders slumped forward quite a bit. It was as if he was exaggerating the bulge that lurked on top of his back. It was much more noticeable than that of a common slouch. This was a little freakish.

"Alright, dude, let's find Ray and get the hell outta here," I ordered.

The three of us snaked our way through the crowds of people, bumping into countless others and picking up unwanted sweat—the downside to all clubs and raves. I spotted Ray off in the distance and sprinted toward him to flee the sauna we were in.

Back on the road, we drove for a short time on an actual highway. When given the order, I veered off into a path that took us into the backwoods of Washington.

"Turn right in here," Jackson guided as he pointed off into a part of the wilderness that apparently contained a trail meant for a car.

My car wasn't the best for getting us to this Embry's house. My poor Firebird was taking a beating up against massive stones partially buried in the hardened dirt. Bushes leaked onto the narrow lane and scraped up against the side doors and fenders. Dust enveloped all around us and made it difficult to see five meters in front of me. Dips and trenches created a loud scratching noise along the guard that hung below the engine, inches above the ground. I wasn't sure how long I could flinch with concern as my car was being beaten.

"Alright, stop right here," Jackson demanded.

I braked and came to a complete stop. I looked through the lighted dust ahead of us only to see trees and shrubs. We were in the middle of nowhere it seemed.

"Stop here?" I questioned. "Where the hell is this place? I don't see a damn thing."

"Yeah, we can't actually drive up to the house," Jackson mentioned. "We gotta cut through these woods for a bit to get there."

What the fuck year was I living in? I thought to myself. This was the 21st century, was it not? Who the hell lives in a place that can't be reached by car? The strangeness of this journey matched the two people Ray and I were with.

All four of us got out of the car and grouped up together.

"We're gonna be on a tiny ass trail with no light, so you guys need to hold on to the back of our shirts as we lead you to the house," Jackson instructed. "Don't let go, or else you guys will get lost. Seriously."

The little light our moon gave off that night was being blocked by the thick cover of forest. There was no penetrating that shelter. It was absolutely pitch black as Ray and I tried to balance ourselves along the thin dirt path. Even after a few minutes of darkness, our eyes seemed useless, unable to adjust to the extreme shade. We blindly held on, inching our way and occasionally getting swatted in the face with a tree branch.

This was truly an eye-opener as I realized how much I took advantage of my sight. They train us briefly on how to deal with incapacitation of our vision in the Army, but during this trek, I gave a deep thought about what it would be like to forever lose my vision. People say if one loses their vision, other senses like hearing and smell are heightened to compensate for the loss. But those who are afflicted with blindness will never be the same, regardless of how well they can see with their hearing or smell.

It took about 15 minutes to reach the front door of Embry's house. This place was completely surrounded by trees and if anyone were to drop dead within the walls of this abode, no search team would be able to spot this residence without the help of advanced technology. The forest canopy even leaked over to cover the top of the house, making it impossible for aircraft to see it from above.

I made myself at home once inside, throwing my body into the couch that sat in the living room. Ray had a seat in the sofa chair which stood next to where I lay.

Embry came over to me with a can of beer in his hand and said in a very low voice, "Here, drink this."

There was something peculiar about the way he said this. His eyes stared along with his blank facial expression. It reminded me of the way a child offers a foe a drink from his cup of soda in which he spit a mouthful of saliva into. Embry gave the can a jerk upward, as if he were taunting me into drinking the contents.

"Here, drink this," he repeated to me.

Cautiously, I reached for the can and snatched it up. I gave him a look and didn't release my stare until he turned back into the kitchen. There was something odd about this guy.

I noticed Jackson speaking to Embry as he entered the kitchen to retrieve a beer. They both spoke rather softly, as if they were trying to hide something. Embry kept a watchful eye, glancing toward Ray and I every few seconds. I would see them cover their mouth now and then, to cover up certain words and phrases. They're going to murder us and bury us on the side of the house, I thought to myself.

I felt as if I should be searching the place for dead bodies, but I didn't want to look too suspicious too soon. I'm sure there was a reasonable explanation for their lunatic ways. Let's give them the benefit of the doubt, I thought.

"Yo, you guys," I hollered toward Jackson and Embry. "Come sit and chill with me and Ray for a minute."

"Yeah, man," Jackson replied. "We'll be there in a minute. We just gotta take care of something."

You gotta figure out where to put the body parts after you sever them off our torsos with a butcher knife, I thought to myself. Or maybe they needed to assign who gets to kill who and in what fashion.

I turned to Ray and whispered to him, "Dude, is it just me, or is there somethin' up with these clowns?"

"Man, I was about to say the same thing," Ray admitted. "These foo's are creepin' me out, man."

"I'm gonna go have a look around for a sec," I whispered to Ray, again giving in to my curiosity.

I turned my voice up and over toward Jackson and Embry and asked, "Hey, where's the bathroom, man. I gotta let some shit flow."

Jackson pointed down a corridor, "Down that hall, to the right. You'll see it," he said.

I reached the lavatory, walked in then closed and locked the door behind me. Everything around me was sparkling with cleanliness. There wasn't a stain to be seen, nor an unsightly watermark anywhere. This place was absolutely spotless. A maid must have just finished tending to the past dirtiness. At least that's how it seemed.

Not only was the bathroom free of any blemishes, but the toiletries inside were amazingly in perfect order and location. I saw the toilet paper hung in its proper overhand fashion, with the next sheet to be taken facing in the most convenient location—facing the toilet. There wasn't a mirrored compartment to keep objects like toothbrushes or razors in. These were rather kept neatly beside the sink. A single, all-white toothbrush laid bristles-up to the left side of the sink with accompanying toothpaste directly next to that. Both appeared to be in mint condition, freshly bought. To the right of the sink was a razor laying in its respective case, neatly positioned at the half-way mark between the faucet and the opposite edge of the sink. Lying behind the razor was, of course, a topped can of shaving gel. At the corner of the sink top, a clean white hand towel was stretched out with various instruments spread upon it, evenly-spaced and all sharing a common grounding. Two pairs of nail clippers—one for the toes and one for the fingers, tweezers, nose hair clippers, dental floss, a tooth scraper and even a nail file were all present. This definitely was not a typical guy's bathroom. The perfection and unfitting uniqueness of all this made the situation even more uncanny. I went back to inform my infantry mate of the circumstances.

"This place is giving me the creeps, dude," I divulged to Ray. "Let's get the hell outta here."

"Yeah, man, for sure," Ray concurred in a slightly panicked voice.

We both got up and walked toward the door. "We're goin' outside to smoke," I called out to Jackson and Embry, who were still in the kitchen, plotting.

Once outside, I turned to Ray and asked, "You remember how to get out of this place?"

"Fuck no!" he exclaimed in fear.

"Alright, alright," I said to Ray, trying to relax his anxiety. "I'm pretty sure the trail was over here in this area."

I pointed off into the dark and began to walk in the direction. I turned out to be correct—I felt the dry dirt of the path underneath my feet as I carefully tried to discern which way to lead. Not much had changed from the previous 30 minutes. The night was still cold and arid. Not one photon of light could be sensed and our surrounding was thick with plantation. My arm was kept stretched out to ward off any stray branches, but the substantial amount of wood and leaves that slapped me in the face was unbearable.

"Dude, I keep getting fucked up by these trees," I said to Ray. "I'm gonna crawl through this shit instead. Hold on to my shoes until we get to the end so you don't get lost."

"Fuck, man," Ray cried. "This is just like work, only I'm not gettin' paid to do this."

I dropped down to my hands and knees and began to crawl like I was on a field problem. I hadn't a clue as to where to go. I did my best to keep above the poorly dug out trail when I suddenly lost the ground from underneath my left knee. Ray's left hand easily slipped from the grasp it had around my ankle as my entire left half of my body dipped down and hung over the edge of a cliff. Rocks tumbled down below into what sounded like a lake. The splashes below sounded like they were about 30 meters away. I kept a strong grip with both my arms and right thigh. In a slow, smooth movement, I pulled the lost portion of my body back up onto the ledge. It was dumb of me to forget this obstacle we experienced on the way to the house.

Ray and I were soon back on track, into the oblivion of the woods. Inch by inch, we slithered our way, staying hopeful we were heading in the correct direction. Even though it took about 15 minutes to get to Embry's house from where my car was parked, it took Ray and me about an hour and a half to finally reach my Firebird. We surely got lost numerous times as we sifted our way, but alas, our chariot to the heavens was unveiled.

"It's about goddamn time!" I exclaimed at first sight of my car.

"Holy fuck!" Ray backed my cry. "I thought we'd never reach civilization again!"

We swiftly jumped into the car and sped off in the direction from which we came. We sped off at a speed of about 10 miles per hour until all natural hardships were out of the way. A paved road was the queue for me to boost our speed to a respectable level. The road we were on didn't seem familiar.

I felt a sharp bump beneath my tires then two seconds later Ray exclaimed, "Oh shiiiiiiiiiiiiiiittt!!" while lifting up the emergency brake with full force and with both his hands clenched around the lever. I could see him using all his strength, pushing his feet into the floor panel.

Naturally, I lifted both my feet and slammed them back down onto the brake and locked my arms straight against the steering wheel to keep it from twisting. The car came to a dramatic stop after sliding for about five seconds.

"Jesus Christ!" I yelled out. "You fuckin' saved our lives!"

I sat, shocked, staring into the lake from the pier on which we now stood. Another four feet and my car would have had to have been dragged out of a lake the next morning.

I couldn't believe that had just happened. My mind was too focused on how strange those two guys we had met were. Every moment spent in their company was extremely awkward. Nothing felt right about them. The feeling is unexplainable. That creepy emotion a person gets when they see a door close by itself during a calm, windless night; that creepy sensation that sends a chill down the spine is what I had felt that night with those two young men—especially Embry. The tone he used when he seldom spoke. The blank stares he gave for no obvious reason. The odd physical features and actions he portrayed. But most importantly, the way he used his eyes to show his emotions was what kept the goose bumps flowing. These types of people are not normal. There was no way they could function correctly in a modern society. Environment and social issues would keep these strangers strange. Ridicule and seclusion would not only segregate these folk into their own grouping, but it would enforce the differences they possessed. This can be a deadly cocktail, creating a monster that must dwell far away from a functioning civilization.

Chapter Thirteen

When I was 19 years old, fresh to Washington, I would often find myself bored during some weekends at the barracks. Playing video games or watching movies on the two days we were free from scrutiny got old rather quickly. At that age, the best thing to do was to flee the country for a couple days to enjoy the brewed sensation of beer. Being in Washington, I didn't have to take a flight or venture off too far from home base to grab a legal drink or two. Canada was only a couple hours away, and with the legal drinking age of 18, it was the hotspot to be like a child in a candy store, only with the candy being beer and the store being bars.

On a Saturday afternoon, I took my friend Gyllis up with me across the border to have fun and drink our cares away. Gyllis was one of the first people I met when I arrived at Fort Lewis. After that night in Canada, we didn't speak to one another much more. Not that he's a jerk or weird. We just didn't click.

Expecting a night of pure drunkenness, I decided to rent a hotel room and leave my car there while Gyllis and I went bar hopping.

The night began early evening, giving us ample time to drench ourselves with alcohol. I must admit that being in the Army—especially Army Infantry—had its perks. A simple mentioning of our jobs and statuses was an automatic invitation for a toast, paid for by civilians. Even in a country I didn't fight for, rounds of beer and shots would be given as a token of worldly appreciation. People understood the hardships I went through, being a grunt. It was their way of saying 'I understand'. And there was never a time I hesitated to tip the bottom of a free drink skyward.

Cheers were chanted and glasses were cracked together throughout that evening. It was a joyous occasion and Gyllis and I had a great time. It was much better than being stuck back at the barracks drinking beer with roommates watching a comedy. We felt like celebrities that night, and the best was still to come, for me.

Unfortunately, the festivities could not go on forever. Although Canada had a lower age limit than the states, the bars weren't paradises. They eventually had to close up and stop the flow of beer.

After closing time, Gyllis and I took a stroll around a block or two, in search of a liquor store to continue the party back at the hotel. Dark streets were all we saw, with no life support to be seen. We had no other choice other than to head back to the hotel room without a case of grog.

Just outside the hotel, I saw a woman talking on a pay phone. She sounded like she was in distress. Her voice was raised with slight anger and she carried a facial expression you never want your girlfriend to have. I couldn't just walk by without getting the full story from this lady. I wanted to see if there was anything I could do for her. Maybe she was left behind and needed a ride back home. Or maybe she just broke up with her husband and needed a non-judgmental ear to speak into. Whatever the case was, I love all women and hate to see one of these goddess-like creatures suffer.

"Yo, man, I'll meet you back at the room," I told Gyllis.

"Yeah, man," he replied back to me. "I'll catch you in a bit."

I walked over to where the woman was standing and reached her just as she slammed the phone back down to disconnect.

"Whoa, whoa, take it easy," I said to her. "I thought the fight was between you and your boyfriend."

"What? You've been eavesdroppin'?" she asked with the angry look still on her face.

"The entire block was eavesdroppin' with you yellin' the way you were just now," I said back to her.

"It wasn't my boyfriend, it was my husband," she admitted, her anger diminishing.

"Sounded like some bad news," I commented.

"Yeah, the usual," she confessed.

"You have a place to go tonight? I've got a room just right here. You should join me," I offered to her.

She paused for a brief moment, searching for the right words to say. "You're hittin' on a 42 year old woman," she revealed.

"What is age other than a number?" I asked, with fireworks going off inside my head.

Before then, I had never slept with a woman much older than me, especially over 20 years older than me.

"Let's go," she told me, taking my hand and walking us inside the hotel.

Score! filled my thoughts. Cheers from all my brain cells fluttered around.

Back at the hotel room, Gyllis started walking out as the 42 year old woman and I were walking in. The two of us went straight for the bedroom, wasting little time. This woman destroyed me. I was far from being a virgin, but she did things to me that no other girl had done to me before. All of those years gave her a generous amount of experience and knowledge that she then shared with me. The way she used her tongue; the amount of body fluid involved; the positions she stretched into; how she vibrated while straddling me; these were all precursors to one of the best sexual occurrences I have ever had.

She was in control during most of the encounter, having me take over only when she was truly out of breath. I'm no smut writer, but I must point out the way she vibrated over me: Toward the middle of the session, I was thrown down to the bed, with my chest facing upward. She slid her dripping pussy over my throbbing cock. I was fully engulfed. She leaned her upper body forward, her perky nipples and b-sized breasts touching my chest. Pushing as far forward as she possible could, she now smashed her breasts against my body. I didn't know it was physically possible for my penis to still be inside of her at that angle, but she was contorted in a way that made sure of it. The small of her back flexed in a way to lift her butt a few inches higher, then back down again. This was the only part of her body that was moving. She was going at a rather fast pace, creating a steady golf clap. Her arms were wrapped around the back of my shoulders, squeezing hard while she kissed the channel created by my collarbone. I had her wrapped in my arms, as well, mending our two bodies into one being. She would pump a few times, and then stop with me fully inside her. When she stopped, she would shake her ass faster than a vibrating sex toy. It was an unbelievable feeling. She shook back and forth as fast as a rattle snake trying to ward off a potential enemy. I was convinced she learned this on some remote island home to people conducting all forms of business in the nude with sex always being the topic discussed and who show their friends appreciation by fixing up orgies. They had taught her well.

I held out as long as I could before I was overwhelmed by the tingling feeling. This occurred when we were doggy style. I pulled out of her and shot my hot rocket fuel all over her face. It was an unprecedented amount for me. I quivered with every spew as she tried to catch as much as she could in her mouth. It did reach her mouth, but every other part of her head, as well, including her eyes, hair and inside her nose. When my eruption was finished, she licked any excess to clean me up. She knew what she was doing.

An overwhelming feeling of satisfaction was seen on both of our faces with grins stretching from ear to ear as we lay there, trying to catch our breath. We lay without saying a word to one another. It was best not to ruin this perfect moment with cheesy remarks. An unprecedented phenomenon had just occurred, and we were well aware of how unique this miracle was.

A few moments had passed, and then the woman sat up and said, "I should get going."

I sat up alongside her and replied, "Ya, sure thing. I'll walk you out."

"Thanks, I'd like that," she said to me with a smile.

She rolled out of the bed and began to gather her clothes. I sat watching her beautiful naked body bend to pick up each article of clothing. This woman was amazing. She definitely did not look her age. In that light, she looked as if she was slightly past the 30 year old mark. Even with her hair tangled like Medusa's snakes, she still turned me on.

After she was completely dressed again, I haphazardly slipped into my jeans and shoes, grabbed my pack of cigarettes with a lighter and helped the lovely lady out of the hotel.

We both smoked a cigarette once outside. Few words were spoken, again. We were still basking in what had just happened.

One thing I do remember her saying to me as she left was, "That was some of the best fucking I have ever had."

That made my night. Hell, that made my month.

Like a teenage boy who just got laid for the first time, I confidently walked back up to my room wearing a bright smile. I surely would have gotten laughed at by anyone who saw me walking by if anyone was even awake at that time.

I got to the room with Gyllis waiting for me. He turned off the television he was watching as I closed the door behind me.

He turned to me and said in a raised voice, "Dude, what the fuck were you doing bringing that chick back here? I was outside waiting forever for you two to finish up!"

"Man, I just had some of the best sex of my life!" I answered him.

"I don't give a fuck, man," he said to me, with full anger in his tone this time. "I'm tired as fuck and I had to wait outside for you."

"Shut the fuck up, man," I said to him, still smiling.

"This aint funny," he said, shaking his head at me.

"Dude, I'm outta here," I said back at him. I grabbed my keys and added, "I'll be sleeping in my car if you need me."

I threw on a brown undershirt and left the hotel room to try to catch a few hours of sleep reclined in the driver's seat of my Firebird. That was easier said than done.

I wasn't quite sure if it was because of the amazing sex I had just had or just the fact that it was a bit uncomfortable, but I couldn't get a second of sleep. I tossed from side to side, sometimes hitting my thigh against the steering wheel, but couldn't get comfortable enough to catch a glimpse of REM. About an hour had passed and light was beginning make itself obvious on the eastern horizon.

It was about five o'clock in the morning when I decided to head back to the states to snooze in the comfort of my own, thin barracks mattress. I was hung over from all the drinking the night before and I started to smell like it. The alcohol began to seep through my pores and it was easily noticeable I had been drinking recently. My eyes were starting to get bloodshot from how tired I was. Just the thought of sleeping all day long once I arrived back to Fort Lewis was orgasmic. I turned the ignition of my car and peeled out of the hotel parking lot.

Vancouver is not very far from the border of the United States and Canada, so it didn't take long for me to reach the quick customs checkpoint on the Interstate 5 highway. But once there, my right foot spent more time on the brake rather than the accelerator. Cars were backed up for what must have been at least a mile. I could barely see the structure that housed the customs agents. I was in no mood for that. I needed to get back home to dream of walking on cotton candy sidewalks and drinking cherry Kool Aid. I teetered back and forth in my seat to see if there was any way out of this mess.

To my left side, I saw a lane with only about three cars lined up. Why the hell is no one using that lane? I asked myself. With my inhibitions still in check, I turned the steering wheel and sped up to the now-vacant gate and stopped behind the lowered bar that prevented cars from speeding past, as if it were made of some super metal. Right when my car came to a complete stop, I looked to my left and saw a customs agent come out of his kiosk with his arms erupting into the air. He was yelling gibberish at me I couldn't understand. His arms were being thrown in the same direction, off to the side of the road. I was finally able to understand all the ranting:

"Get the hell to the side of the road!" he screamed at me.

The bar was raised for me to drive through only to pull over to the side of the road.

Shit. This can't be good, I thought to myself. I smell of booze and that lane I just drove in probably wasn't meant for me.

The customs agent ran over to my driver's side window. I rolled it down to hear him yell at me, "Why the hell are you driving in the import/export lane?"

"Clearly you are not authorized to utilize that lane," he went on to explain. "Only vehicles with the proper certification can use that lane for quick access to and from both countries. I need you to step out of your vehicle and come with me," he said as he then gestured with his hands to shut off the car engine.

I did as he ordered and began to walk over to the office that was located at the far end of all the incoming lanes. As I walked, I took deep breaths and tried to gain composure. It was quite obvious I was still drunk and I didn't want to make things worse than they already were. I patted down my arms and legs, as if the drunkenness and tiredness could simply be washed away. My eyes gave a few strong blinks, to pump some life back into them.

My driver's license was immediately asked for after I stepped inside the small room. Without hesitation and as fluidly as I could, I presented the identification card.

"So, you want to explain yourself," an officer sitting behind a desk asked me as he peered down at my license, "Mr. Stiles?"

"Sir, I had no idea," I began to give my spiel. "This was the first time I have been to Canada and I was not aware that such a lane existed. I looked over to the lane and saw vehicles proceeding through the gate and thought it would be fine for me to enter," I tried to explain as properly as possible.

"It wasn't until I saw your officer that I knew I was in the wrong. I am fully aware of the usage of the lane in question now and I can guarantee to you that I will never enter it again if I should enter or exit Canada in the future," I did my best not to breathe heavily as I spoke, to conceal the smell of booze.

"You're damn right you won't ever do this again," the agent said to me. "I'm entering your name and vehicle license plate number into our database. If anyone ever catches you in that lane again, you will be arrested on the spot, without question. Am I making myself clear, Mr. Stiles?"

"Yes, sir," I replied to his simple question, "absolutely, sir."

"Now get the hell outta here," he handed my driver's license back to me and pointed to the door.

"Yes, sir," I acknowledged. "Sorry to cause any inconvenience to you, sir," my formal tongue was still in action.

I slipped out of there as fast as I could and was well on my way back home before I gave a second thought as to what had just occurred.

Over the years I learned how to con—or talk—my way out of certain situations. That time at the border of Canada and the United States should have wound up with me getting at least a fine of some sort. I was there, a mess, drunk, and in the wrong but was still able to peacefully find my way out. A mutual understanding of respect between all parties is what is needed in most cases to be set free. If you are in trouble at any point in your life and you need to explain your way out, like after getting caught cheating on your girlfriend or after completely mishandling a business presentation, if you are able to show you respect the other person(s)' opinions and thoughts, and if you are able to do this so they gain your respect, then an agreement or compromise should rise from the situation. Believe it or not, making others feel important is like a get-out-of-jail-free card. One can get away with murder as long as they present the case in an orderly fashion to gain admiration by their peers. And if that doesn't work, play the sympathy card. The sympathy card came in handy for me during an errand run for a friend of Sophia's.

Sophia's friend, Alice, wanted to stock up on some ecstasy pills one winter. Maybe she thought the suppliers dried up along with the trees every year. Alice wanted to buy 100 pills from a supplier that lived in the woods of Washington. But she didn't want to risk getting caught, so basically Sophia 'volun-told' me to help her friend out by picking the pills up for her. Sophia and I set out after we received the money from Alice.

The supplier truly was in the woods of Washington. It was difficult to find our way there. Some of the roads leading to the rundown cottage that housed the junkie weren't even paved. But this was normal for Washington. What wasn't normal was the smell that came from within that shack of a house we found ourselves in. We spent little time inside to snatch up the pills and quickly bid our leave.

The ride back to Fort Lewis from the supplier was longer than it took to get to the supplier from Fort Lewis. Obviously, we were lost. The cherry on top of the cake came when flashing police lights popped up in my rear view mirror.

The situation was this: it was me and Sophia, lost in the winding back roads of the wilderness. We had 100 ecstasy pills in the trunk of my car. The car's registration was expired—come to think of it, I don't think I ever once renewed the registration the entire time I owned the Firebird. I had no car insurance. I was also driving without any identification, let alone a driver's license. There were multiple things that could have put me away, including a felony possession with possible intent to distribute.

"Officer, I'm really sorry," I began to explain with the police man standing outside of my rolled-down window. "Me and my girlfriend are lost and we're trying to find our way back to the main highway. I'm not from this area. I just moved up here, into Fort Lewis. I'm in the Army Infantry. Could you please just give us a warning just this once. All we're trying to do is get back to my base so I can get some rest before I have to work early tomorrow."

"Army Infantry, eh," the officer said to me.

"Yes, sir," I replied to him. "I'm in the 132nd Airborne," I said to him. That was the first number that popped into my head.

Hesitantly, the cop said to me, "Alright, I'm going to let you go with a warning. I need you to try to drive more safely down these tricky roads. I don't want you to get into an accident."

He pointed back toward his police cruiser that stood behind my car. "The main highway is back that way, not too far. Make a right turn at the second intersection," he instructed.

I nodded and said, "Thanks a lot, officer."

Slowly, I made a u-turn and fled the scene, unscathed. Piece of cake, I thought.

On a separate occasion, I found myself driving home from a house party that a sergeant of my platoon threw one Saturday night. Dirty Duncan was riding in the back seat of my car. Again, we were both quite drunk from a night full of debauchery, drinking and fighting with ketchup bottles. Yeah, you read correctly—ketchup bottles. I distinctly remember this because my shirt was littered with ketchup stains which looked as if I had gotten into a brawl and had my opponent's blood splattered all over me. I honestly couldn't tell you how Army Infantry soldiers began squirting ketchup at one another. It's quite possible my subconscious intentionally blocked that part of the story out for fear of word spreading.

Duncan and I sped down a highway on our way home when the usual colorful lights began to flicker behind us. As I grew older, I realized this was only usual for me, it seemed. Talking to some friends and family later in my life made me aware that I had gotten pulled over by law enforcement an awful lot. I run into people time and time again who have never been pulled aside by a police officer. I don't know—maybe I have just been lucky.

"Ah, shit!" Dirty shrieked out. "We're gonna get fucked for underage drinking!"

I left out that small detail. We were both underage at the time. So far, I was driving drunk as a minor.

"Yeah, this aint lookin' good," I admitted to Duncan, trying to keep my cool. "This car isn't insured or registered. And I guess I should have brought my driver's license, eh?"

Driving an unregistered vehicle, drunk, with no insurance or license as a minor.

"Dude, I'm gonna pretend to be passed out back here so he doesn't catch me," Duncan explained to me. "Don't say anything to me when he comes up here."

"What the fuck, man," I said towards the back seat. "You're gonna let me take this all by myself?"

My car slowly came to a stop on the side of the highway.

"I can't hear you," Dirty said to me, "I'm asleep."

I looked in my rear view mirror to see Duncan slouch way down in his seat and hang his head down so his chin touched the top of his chest. He had one eye open and smiled at me as I glared at him in the mirror.

"Fuck, man, whatever," I gave in to him.

The officer parked his police cruiser behind my car. A few seconds passed then I saw him step out of his vehicle and start walking toward my rolled-down window.

"Do you know why I pulled you over?" the officer asked me after he reached my door.

I looked at him with bright eyes and replied, "No, sir. What did I do wrong?"

"You were speeding 15 miles over the limit," he announced. "I clocked you going 80 in a 65 mile an hour zone."

Speeding an unregistered vehicle, drunk, with no insurance or license as a minor.

I cleared my throat to make my words as audible as possible. "I'm really sorry, officer. I'm just trying to make it back to my base to catch some sleep. I'm really tired."

My eyes glanced up to the rear view mirror to see Duncan peering through a sliver created by his eyelids to see what was happening up front. The officer caught my glimpse and bent over to have a look for himself.

"Is your friend okay back there?" he asked me.

My eyes flew to the right then back towards the police officer. "Yeah, he's fine," I said to the uniformed man. "He's just really tired."

The cop stood back up. "You also have a broken tail light," he continued to deliver.

Speeding an unregistered vehicle with a broken tail light, drunk, with no insurance or license as a minor.

"You boys get into some trouble tonight?" the officer asked me with his eyes locked on the red ketchup stains on my shirt.

"It's a long story, sir," I said with a slight laugh, shaking my head with embarrassment. "It's actually just ketchup."

Speeding an unregistered vehicle with a broken tail light, drunk, with no insurance or license, wearing a ketchup-stained shirt as a minor.

"You said you're heading back to base? Fort Lewis?" he asked me.

"Yes, sir," I replied.

The officer squinted his eyes at me and said, "I could impound this unregistered vehicle right now if I wanted to."

He placed both his hands on the car door and said the magic words that made everything better, "But I'm going to let you boys go."

"Oh! Thank you so much, officer!" a scream came from the back seat.

My eyes shut tightly and my head dropped. The officer's eyes and head swung to have a look at a 'freshly napped' Duncan.

Keep your fucking mouth shut, Dirty! I exclaimed to myself. We're almost completely out of the woods with this one.

My head flew up in an instant. My eyebrows propped high to vividly expose the whites of my eyes and I uttered out to the officer, "Have a great night, sir!"

He stepped back and I hastily started my car and drove out of there.

Chapter Fourteen

Imagine walking to your car one morning to head off to the office where you work, with a cup of coffee in one hand and a set of fumbling keys in the other. Still tired from a terrible night's sleep atop a mattress that seemed to be constructed of splintered plywood, you jostle the longest key into the door panel to open the hatch which leads to a staunch smell of still water. You nestle your body into the cold leather seats to ready yourself for the 30 minute ride to work. Another turn of the key to start the engine, you back out of the driveway and begin to head down your street.

It is still much too early for the clamoring of energetic disc jockeys to be broadcasted from the car speakers, so you sit, quietly and slowly rolling down the hill on which your house sits. You look to your left in disgust to see a jogger in full attire running alongside her gracious dog. You think to yourself, how the fuck can someone purposely wake up at this time? How the hell can they wake up at a time that is practically non-existent to me and do something that requires energy and willpower?

Your face loathingly shrivels as you stare. Then you turn your attention back to the front of your car. You continue driving, at a minimal speed. Just like you, your vehicle needs plenty of time to warm up to its full potential. Automatically, you turn the steering wheel a bit to the right, to brush up close to the parked cars on the side of the road. A squint is made by your eyelids, but only to try to catch the detail of the object that you see in the center of the street. It seems as if a massive tree had sprouted from asphalt in the past night. This thick tree was painted all around and was carved to resemble a person dressed in a ceremonial garb. The arms and legs that were sliced from this tree trunk weren't sticking out like branches, but rather were placed in a fashion that had the statue remain a consistent thickness from top to bottom. What you see is a totem pole a person would see on an Indian reservation.

You slowly roll towards it with your eyes releasing the squints. A blank look comes across your face as you near the figure. No new thoughts come to mind. No questions come to mind. Your head turns, with your stare still locked on its target as you and your car drive by. You come to the stop sign where you subsequently hop onto the main road to catch the highway leading to your job. Like nothing strange had occurred, you go about your day just like any other.

I can almost guarantee an experience very similar to the one I just described happened one morning in the city of Bremerton, Washington.

Bremerton was the home of a nearby naval base, and it was also home of an ongoing joke the soldiers had in Fort Lewis. We claimed women who came from that area had only one body type. The body type could be easily compared to a buffalo's. We thought women there were overweight and hairy. This gave rise to the pet name 'bremaloes'. Because of it being a grazing haven for these bremaloes, Bremerton was also a hot spot for me and some Army friends to go 'hogging'. Hogging is a competition. A group of guys would get together and go out for a night at the clubs or bars. Each guy would try to pick up a girl from one of these joints who had bremalo status. The man who brought back the biggest bremalo to their place would be the winner. And I use the term 'winner' extremely loosely.

Hogging filled up an evening for me and three of my Army friends, Stan, Iric, and Joe. It was a boring Saturday night so we decided to throw in 50 dollars apiece to see who can get the biggest bremalo out of the four of us. We were soon in my car and off to Bremerton.

We decided to go to a bar instead of a club, knowing we would probably need an abundant supply of alcohol to make the process easier. Granted, the club scene had little light for us to see exactly what we would be getting into, but it was a unanimous decision.

We pulled up to a dive bar that had the look of being a bremalo sanctuary. The four of us walked inside and our instincts were correct. Rolls of flabbiness were everywhere within the small bar. It was as if the walls, floors and stools were growing a bloated, oversized fungus. I wanted to hold my breath the entire time I was there to protect my lungs from getting infected. Many of the women clung on to the arms of normal-sized men, afraid of letting their catch wander off to another woman that looked less like cotton candy and more like a straw of candied sugar. The four of us were the most athletic and handsome men in the room. This is going to be too easy, I thought to myself.

"Alright, guys, let's get to work," I said with a smile on my face.

"I call that one over there," Iric said to the other three of us as he pointed toward the back of the bar.

"Every man for themselves from here on out," Stan set out the rules.

I saw a good-sized girl ordering a drink at the bar. I decided to try to make the best out of the evening.

"Hey, beautiful," I said to the girl. "Are you buying a drink for me?"

She turned to look at me and quickly began to blush. Her head tilted slightly down and her eyes looked in many different directions, unable to focus on a particular object.

"Uuuh-uh, uh," she stuttered out. "Uh, yeah, of course!"

She finally made eye contact with me and asked, "What do you drink?"

"You can get me a Bud on tap," I told her.

"Ok, yeah, sure thing," she continued to show her nervousness.

She turned to the bartender and said, ". . . and a tall Bud on tap."

I'm not a completely shallow person. In all circumstances, I try to find the best things a person may possess. And after the first few seconds with this girl, I found something she had going for her. She actually had a pretty face. She had long, loosely curled sexy hair that flowed down the sides of a pretty, fat face.

"So, why don't you tell me your name, gorgeous," I said to her.

"Uh, um," a bright smile formed after some stuttering. "My name is Brianna."

"Brianna," I said back to her, with a twinkle shining from one of my teeth. "That's a cute name. My name's Gino."

"Hi, Gino," she said to me and held out her hand for me to shake.

I swooped her hand up to my lips and gave the backside a soft kiss and smiled.

"It's a pleasure," I said to her, still smiling and still putting on the charm for an easy lure.

And it turned out to be just that. It only took two drinks that were watered down with my cheesy compliments to convince her to invite me to her place for the night.

"I see your friend over there talking to one of my friends," Brianna told me, nodding her head in the direction in which Stan was talking up another bremalo.

"Do you two want to go home with us?" she asked.

I cocked my head and put a confused look on my face. I was unsure how she knew Stan was my friend. Brianna noticed my uncertainty.

"I saw you walk in with him," she said to me, putting my mind at ease.

"Oh, I see," I responded. "Yeah, let's get outta here and go have some fun at your place. I'll go grab my buddy."

I purposely said that so I could get out of paying the bar tab.

"Hey, man, who's your lovely friend?" I asked Stan as I approached him and his newly captured bremalo.

"This is Janet," Stan told me.

Before my friend could give my disguise away by introducing me to Janet, I stepped in and did it for him.

"Hi, Janet," I said to her. "My name's Gino. I've been talking to your friend over there, Brianna, and she wants all of us to head back to her place for a drink or two."

"Oh, that sounds nice," Janet said to me. "Good thing, too, I'm actually getting a bit tired. I didn't get much sleep last night. I had to wake up early this morning-"

"Interesting story, dear," I interrupted her story. "I'll have my buddy here fill me in on the details later. We should get going."

The four of us gathered and headed out of the bar to my Firebird. Iric and Joe will surely find a safe ride home, I convinced myself.

The ride to Brianna's home was quiet and slightly awkward. The longest conversation was all about how exactly to get to the house. I guess it was kind of difficult to find a topic to talk about without a drink in our hands.

We arrived at Brianna's house with her friend Janet passed out asleep in the back seat. Jokingly, I said to Stan, "Don't wake her. Just carry her inside."

Stan whispered back to me, "Yeah, let me just call in our medical helo to air lift this monster out of the car."

Stan gave Janet a few taps on the shoulder. She awoke after about the 10th one.

"Come on," Stan said to her. "Let's head inside."

Wiping away a drop of drool, Janet stumbled out of the car, quickly walked through the door to Brianna's house and took a dive onto the couch just beyond the main entrance. Brianna, Stan and I followed behind and sat on sofa chairs surrounding the couch.

Another awkward silence started to build up when Brianna stood up and said to me and Stan, "I gotta go to the bathroom. You guys make yourselves comfortable. If you want a drink, there's some liquor in the kitchen over there," she pointed deeper into the house.

Stan and I sat there, still in silence, until Brianna was out of sight, then I uttered, "Dude, I totally won!"

"No way!" Stan yelled at me. "Do you see the size of this girl?! She must weigh 400 pounds!"

"Man, two of yours wouldn't equal close to one of mine!" I exclaimed.

"Haha, whatever, dude," Stan said. "Let's just get the fuck out of here."

"Yeah, for sure," I began to say. "But hold on. Let's fuck with this fat ass first."

I looked around the room for ideas. I walked over to a desk that stood in the far corner of the room. I rifled through some papers and books but only found a black marker pen that would be useful to me.

"I'm gonna write on this chick's face," I told Stan. "You go start grabbin' some of that liquor she was talkin' about."

I stood above Janet's sleeping body for a second to examine what I should write. I then leaned down to her face and drew the letter 'c' above her left eye, another letter 'c' below her left eye, and a letter 'k' below the previous 'c'. Next, I completely filled both of her upper eyelids with the black ink. Then, I drew the letter 'p' above her right eye, an 'o' below her right eye, and another letter 'p' below the 'o'. To this day, I still think the word 'poop' is hilarious. After that, I went ahead and filled in her uni-brow.

Stan walked back in the room with seven liquor bottles in his arms.

"Cool, let's get the fuck outta here," he said to me.

"Let's roll!" I confirmed.

We began to head towards the front door when I glanced to the far left of the room. I stopped, and my entire body paused for a few seconds as I stared at one of the strangest things I had ever seen. It was unbelievable how neither I nor Stan saw the massive object that sat there watching over us as we lay comfortable on the sofa chairs. The shear girth of the thing took up the size of a coffee table.

It was a tall-standing totem pole. Staring at it, I couldn't tell if the face was smiling or grinning. The pole seemed quite special—the way it was painted and detailed—which made me think it was used for some certain rituals at one point. One thing came to mind as I faced the totem.

"Dude!" I broke my trance. "I gotta take that thing!"

"What the fuck is it?" Stan asked me with a disgusted face.

"I don't know, but that shit's coming with us in the trunk," I answered.

"Hurry up, then," Stan said as he made his way out the door.

It took all my strength to not only get the totem pole out of the house, but to lift it into the trunk and backseats of my car. It was rather unstable and I was very unsure about driving with that thing in my car. The round body made it easy for it to roll around and cause some damage to my car.

Just like a mother leaving a newborn child on the doorstep of an unfamiliar house, I had to make the difficult decision to part ways with my pole.

Chapter Fifteen

Now, imagine driving along a busy highway, going about 65 miles an hour. You are a retired Colonel of the Army and you're off to visit a close family friend who lives on the other side of town. You live in a quiet suburb of Baton Rouge, Louisiana and you spend most of your free time with your grandchildren, living a simple life in a nice house. You try to stay away from the little drama your beautiful wife creates being the only member of the family who still has a full time job teaching at the local primary school.

It is a warm, humid day. The thermometer isn't high enough to drive with the air conditioning turned on, so you have your windows rolled slightly down. It is midday and there are beautiful puffy white clouds in the sky. They peacefully float by, giving no indication of rain or other ailments. Trees towards your right sway rhythmically without missing a step. It is a completely wonderful day.

A faddish, no-rules radio station is heard on your car stereo. It is the type that plays a wide variety of music. From classic rock to modern pop to alternative to indie to bands that almost cross the line into the punk genre, the DJ plays just about everything that can be broadcasted on popular radio stations—except country. No one likes country.

Your fingers tap the 10 and 2 positions of the steering wheel to try to go along with a new Linkin Park song. It is new to your ears, but the beat and melody is very catchy. You feel as if you are with the in-crowd, listening to one of the vocalists rap along. Besides you bobbing your head up and down to the New Age hit, nothing is out of the ordinary—until you look over to the other side of the road.

A small caravan of three futuristic looking, half monster truck half tank resembling vehicles come slowly roaring by the expressway. They are getting easily passed up by the miniature sedans and SUV's that normally travel this course. The behemoths are a dark grayish color with three massive wheels on both the starboard and port side. There isn't an obvious offensive capability. No barrels or tactical weapons can be seen. The vehicles don't look quite like a tank, but they also don't look quite like anything you have ever seen in the 20 years of Army service. It is like a scene out of a science fiction movie. The picture is both interesting and unsettling. You wonder why the hell these things are on the road.

About an hour before the Colonel's sighting, me and my team of 13 other infantry soldiers were readying our leave to head back to our home base of Fort Lewis, Washington. We were called to duty in the outskirts of Louisiana to test out a new, advanced form of technology the Army was about to unveil to the troops who were now fighting in Afghanistan and Iraq. This technology was called the Striker. It was an attack vehicle which had bomb-resistant armor, camouflaged anti-tank weapons and was able to house up to 8 soldiers within it. It was highly advanced and I'm afraid to give much more details about the vehicle itself.

Our test runs were finished up and my team was loading up the vehicles onto a trailer to be sent off to the nearby Army base. We had been working all day long to get the final tests completed and we were all a bit tired from the rush.

"Hey, Sergeant," one of my men called over to me.

At the time of this operation, I was at the rank of Sergeant and was able to oversee a small group of soldiers.

"Yeah, what's up, Milik?" I asked.

"We're all a bit hungry and some soldiers from the other squad were sayin' that there's a Burger King just down the road there," Milik began to explain. "Is it cool if one of us goes for a run?"

"Yeah, man," I answered him. "Just be back quick. I'm hungry."

"Alright, cool," Milik said back to me.

I sat down on a makeshift bench to close up the final parts of the paperwork involved with the tests. I basically had to make sure to report any faults, if any, the vehicles had as we underwent the rigorous examination. I needed to confirm whether or not the Strikers were ready for issue.

About five minutes of writing had passed and I looked up to see Milik still assisting with the loading of the Strikers.

"Yo, Milik!" I yelled out to him. "I'm starvin'! When are you headed out for Burger King?"

He ran over to me with bad news.

"Sarge, we don't have a car to borrow to get down there," he said to me.

"Damn!" I said out loud. "You got me all excited for some burgers."

Milik turned to go back to the group to continue to help. Before he could take a step back, I said to him, "Hold up, hold up. Let me think a sec."

I raised my right hand to grab a hold of my chin while I had some thoughts fly through my head. My eyes narrowed and my head went from side to side.

I finally said to Milik with a smile on my face, "I'll tell you what. Before you guys load up those three Strikers, there, take those to grab some food for everyone."

With his eyebrows raised, Milik questioned my decision in a high pitched voice, "Are you sure we can do that?"

"Yeah, dude," I replied to him. "Don't worry, I got your back. Just bring me back a large combo meal with a Coke."

I went back to finishing up the paperwork.

My food hadn't even arrived back to me when I heard the Staff Sergeant who was overlooking the Striker group process yell for me. He didn't sound too happy.

"Stiles!!!" I heard the voice cry out.

"Over here, Staff Sergeant," I called back to him, already knowing what this was going to be about.

"Where the fuck are your Strikers?!" the yelling continued.

"They should be gettin' me some food," I said to the Staff Sergeant in a smart way.

"Holy fuck, Stiles!" A short pause, then, "This is comin' down from the general himself! Some old retired Colonel called in to complain to the General of the base. That shit snowballed all the way to here and it's about to hit a fuckin' tree!"

"You better be glad your ass is leavin' today or you'd be in for some real shit, Stiles!" the Staff Sergeant roared. "Expect to get your ass kicked once you get back to your base. I'm gonna go write a detailed report that will have your ass!"

In a puff of smoke, the Staff Sergeant was gone and it was the last that I heard of the situation. By that time, I had built up so many friends back at Fort Lewis and I had so many connections that no repercussions were administered to me after I got back to base. I knew all the right people and I stayed away from the right people. I could have gotten away with murder if I really wanted to. I was the best at what I did and everyone knew and respected that fact. Throughout my Army career, I outshined just about everyone I encountered. Infantrymen who had served for over 15 years were getting schooled by me. My field performances were flawless and needed little training.

I had a very cocky attitude whilst in the Army. But that was because I had earned it. My chin was carried up high with my chest boldly sticking outward because I knew I was the best. It was a fine line between love and hate with those who overlooked me. My instructors and squad leaders loved that I did my tasks so perfectly. But they hated the attitude that went along with perfection. Most were able to accept the positives and drowned out the negative. Those were the ones who I had a mutual respect for. I admired those who admired and understood me. I admired those who weren't afraid to ask me for my help when they needed it. I made them realize I was always there to lend a hand. And for those who couldn't accept the way I was in the Army, I didn't even need to know they existed. These qualities are still true to this day.

Chapter Sixteen

It goes without saying a few of the things I have done in my past are simply silly and haven't taught me much, but I have been in numerous situations that have given me useful insight and experience that comes in handy at my job as a Deputy Sheriff. It is proven to me on a daily basis while working at the station that most other deputies are very inexperienced and they really don't belong on the force. Deputy Sheriffs are supposed to be separate from civilians; they are supposed to uphold the law and to protect and serve the average civilian. But to me, there is a copious amount of law enforcement officers that are civilians in my eyes. They have no right to wear a uniform that boasts otherwise.

A perfect example of this was on a night I was on duty at a jail. Once hired as a Deputy Sheriff in California, the cop needs to spend 2 years working in the jails before they are based at an actual department to patrol. I actually bypassed most of the jail time for something a lot more posh. It happened when I had gotten into an argument with a female colleague at work. I was basically trying to explain to her she was stupid and didn't know anything about anything. I was later proven to be correct and for my reward, I was transferred to stand duty at a county hospital rather than the jails.

But I digressed.

I was on duty with this obvious rookie, named Higgins. He had just gotten back from doing a walkthrough of the cells to make sure everything was orderly.

"Stiles," he took my attention away from the newspaper I was reading. "I smell weed in the halls. You wanna come with me to do a cell check?"

"What you smell is not weed, Higgs," I replied back to him. "All it is is tobacco."

"I know what cigarettes smell like, Stiles," he said back to me with a discerning face.

"Dude, you're not gonna waste my time with this," I said to Higgins, flipping through another page in the newspaper. "It's just tobacco."

"It's not tobacco, I guarantee it," he said.

"And I guarantee it is. If you're so sure, make it worth my while to get up out of this chair and put 100 bucks on it," I wagered.

"Alright, fucker, let's go do the check," he accepted.

I threw my newspaper down and got up from my chair. We headed to the second floor of the jail block to where he smelt the source of the 'weed'. I already knew the smell was of tobacco, I took a feint whiff of it from downstairs. But this was an easy way to make 100 extra dollars.

We got to the cell and had it opened.

Higgins placed handcuffs on the prisoner and ordered him not to move in the corner of the cell, "Get over there and don't fuckin' move a muscle."

We began our search by looking in the usual spots, like under the bed, blankets, pillows and in the toilet. Prisoners weren't dumb enough to leave things like that lying around, but all bases need to be covered when doing something like this. Plus, it gave us time to think about all other possible hiding places.

Nothing came up until I threw the pillow from the bed onto the floor. I could hear a feint sound of a plastic baggy as it hit the ground. Jackpot.

I knelt down for further examination and felt the obvious lump inside the pillow. Upon further assessment, I noticed a small hole on the side of the pillow where the baggy would be slipped in. I dug in and retrieved a small bag of tobacco along with a lighter and some small paper squares used for cigarette casings.

I held out the bag above my head, still kneeling down, and said to Higgins, "It looks as if I'm 100 dollars richer, pal."

I turned my head to see Higgins wasn't immediately convinced.

"Can you not tell from there?" I asked him in disbelief.

He came in for a closer look and said, "Let me check."

Before he could get too close, I tossed the bag at him angrily. I was reminded of the trouble we had just gone through due to the lack of knowledge.

"God dammit, Higgs," I said in a disappointed tone. "You gotta know these things."

This was exactly the thing that made me feel I was so much far ahead of other deputies. Most others were still in the high school of experience and I was well past my university graduation. It is quite embarrassing to see this happen time and time again on the force.

Another thing that sometimes makes me hate admitting I am a cop is when I see another police officer scared of a situation they should be able to handle on their own. These officers, again, are trained to combat any dangerous situation they may face in the line of duty. They have the skills and tools necessary to tackle most hazards, from bomb threats to suicide attempts to robberies to well-armed hostage circumstances.

While working in the jails, we would escort prisoners to various places throughout the complex, depending on what the occasion was. I would be asked the same question over and over again by my colleagues: "Why do you never use the waist chains that we provide? Why do you rarely handcuff the prisoners?"

I think cops take entirely too much precaution in what they do. They do this because they are scared to engage any action that might be considered to be harmful. I am very confident in everything I do, and to be honest, I sometimes wish a prisoner or suspect *does* try to take me on. This may sound a bit odd, but I think it would be fun to have a suspect try to flee or try to reach for my gun to make an escape to freedom. I would give anything to be in that situation! The whole element of danger is why I decide to go to work every day. I wish a scary incident would unravel so it would make it worthwhile to continue doing what I do. I often find it extremely boring working as a police officer and need a boost of adrenaline in order to not become a zombie.

While on duty, I don't even wear my bullet proof vest that was issued to us. Working on the streets of Los Angeles, it is almost a unanimous consensus to wear the protection. But there are two reasons why I prefer to not to wear the fortification. The first is, again, the whole element of danger thing. The second is a comfort issue. I find myself inhibited whilst wearing it. If I ever find myself in the situation where I would need the support of a bullet proof vest (oh, how I wish), then I would much rather have the mobility to get a shot from my Beretta a half of a second faster than I would be able to while wearing the vest. Timing plays a more crucial role when live fire is being exchanged. Spending time in the Army has cemented this idea into my head.

Up until the time I actually became a deputy, I had spent time in a cell, behind bars. I had not only fled from a police cruiser, but I had escaped from the hot pursuit. I had been part of countless drug deals and been the dealer himself. I had been to countless broken up parties. I had been in a courtroom setting on numerous occasions to defend my freedom. I had frequently gotten my way out of citations that would be issued to me after being pulled over by police officers. I had experienced the effects of various drugs first hand and know exactly what they are capable of doing to the human body and psyche. I had stolen items from unsuspecting people. I had met people who appeared to literally be insane. I had met people who could easily be taken advantage of. I had learned who to trust and who not to trust. I had learned how to tell if someone is lying or telling the truth. I'm far more skilled than what my resume may declare.

Chapter Seventeen

One thing I'm very tired of is the politics that surround the workplace. They are especially prevalent in government jobs like law enforcement and the military, but come on! I thought deputies would be a lot more professional than they actually are, but this is not the case at all. It's all about who you know or who you sleep with. It's rarely about how well you do your job or about how much skill you have. If a deputy is good at pleasing the Sheriff or pleasing those above him in the chain of command (i.e. kissing ass), then he can go far in his career. If you have the right connections, you will do well on the force. Which brings us to how I got this job in the first place.

Like the aforementioned, I don't think I should be a Deputy Sheriff. It is hard to imagine that I squeaked by the radar. Yes, I have a blood relative who is well-respected on the police force. He has been on duty for over 20 years and knows his job inside and out. He's a brilliant man and I owe lots to him. With my connection to him and with his connections within the departments, I was able to have some things that happened in my past overlooked. During the hiring process, I was able to be interviewed with members who were in cahoots with my situation. Every part of my hiring was thought out in advance and success was ensured. I hate to sound like I'm blaspheming and contradicting myself, but when an opportunity like this presents itself to you, you got to take advantage. Besides, this is much different from ass-kissing to get what you want. And I'll show you the difference.

My insider never really got the high rank he deserved. The reason he didn't is because he doesn't kiss ass. Again, this man knows the law as if he was struck over the head one day and instead of being able to recite any mathematical problem in the same time it takes to blink an eye, all the knowledge of police codes, police etiquette, what to do and what not to do in every situation while in the line of duty and every possible police experience was implanted into his brain. This man is one of the smartest people I know, and he shows it in his work. But unfortunately, his knowledge has never gotten recognized by those who controlled the promotions.

The groups of cops who my insider *does* work with respect him to the fullest because they *do* recognize the accomplishments. At any point they need advice about what to do or the procedures for a certain circumstance, they don't hesitate to ask my helper. He's quite a popular person in the department, but not for his social skills—which he lacks. Well, it's not that he lacks social skills, but it's more that he speaks his mind much too often, which can sometimes be funny. And he sometimes runs away and gets very much into various stories he carried out on duty. But it is this social misunderstanding that also has created a barrier to not allow him to reach the rank he deserves. Nevertheless, he has gotten respect, which is more important.

With this wonderful source leading me to a position as a Deputy Sheriff, it may sound like it was a piece of cake to get hired. But that statement is far from reality. We had to jump through so many hoops to bypass all the accusations my past had encountered. It was a painful and time-consuming process. I had a possible domestic violence charge to battle with. I had driving under the influence charges. My name and vehicle license plate has been recorded into an incalculable amount of databases.

During one stage of the hiring process for all would-be police officers and deputies, the applicants must be examined by a polygraph test. Polygraphs, or lie detectors, are very questionable pieces of equipment. They no longer hold up in the court of law and there are methods to successfully lie to the lie detector without being caught. A polygraph's sensors are hooked up to different parts of the body to measure fluctuations in body temperature, heartbeat and muscle tension. Recordings are made after each question asked to compare to what is called the baseline. The baseline is determined by the initial questions asked to the person being tested. These are simple questions that are obvious to both parties. For example, 'Is your name Frank Stiles?'

or 'Do you reside in Los Angeles?'. The answers to these questions will—or should—create the bodily conditions that will exist for all true answers. If a contestant lies, these conditions should change. It's human nature to act slightly different when a lie is being told.

The problem with polygraphs lies in the baseline. If it doesn't have a proper baseline, or the results generated from the baseline questions are inaccurate, then the entire procedure will simply be a small interrogation. And there are a few different ways to manipulate the machine to your advantage. The most common method is to have a thumbtack positioned inside your shoe to strike your toe if you press down upon it. You would do this after each question, so every answer has a rise in heart palpitations and emotion from the pain caused. With this method, no baseline would be acquired.

But the technique I used was much different. Drugs. If you calm the body to a certain point, then it will be unable to show measureable changes in conditions. A drug of choice for most is valium. Valium puts the body in a very relaxed state, creating the perfect circumstances for manipulating the machine. But I chose a lesser known drug to aid my inaccurate readings. I heard of a drug called phenibut from a friend. Phenibut has similar effects to valium, but it's much easier to get. Most bodybuilding websites or retailers carry the powder. A difference between valium and phenibut is the latter also puts you in a focused state. If a task is to be completed, phenibut makes sure all your brainpower is geared towards the completion of the task. My friend introduced it to me as well as others who were finishing their studies in colleges or universities.

But even with some covert operations to ease my way through the system, my knowledge of someone on the department turned out to benefit me in a fantastic way. I guess some of the politics seen in the workforce can be tolerated.

But something I can't stomach is the true answer behind a common question asked about cops by civilians: whether or not police officers lie to get convictions. It was sickening when I found out that just about every officer twists the truth when writing reports in ways to get the charges against suspects. The more and more I talked to the different cops on duty, the more they admitted to doing such things. I can't imagine exactly how many convicted criminals are actually innocent. They're probably not fully innocent, but surely not guilty enough to be locked up for longer than they should be.

When I worked in the cells, it was rather common to hear an inmate declare their innocence. Now I wonder . . .

People would ask me all the time, "How could you work with these bad men? Some of them are murderers, child molesters, rapists . . ."

Shocked faces resulted when I told them, "Well, I can actually sympathize and sometimes even empathize with some of these people."

"I mean, these people are in jail now. They're not out killing others or raping little kids anymore. They're human beings. Sure, they did something wrong in their past, but they're obviously not doing it anymore."

And it is because of this I treat the inmates right. If they show me respect and don't try to mess with me, then I'm going to do the same with them. If they do as I say without getting an attitude and without hassle, then I'm not going to cause more hardships and pain than they already experience. Again, these people *are* people.

Although, I can't say I have the same sympathy or empathetic feelings for some of my colleagues. I have witnessed brutality and physical harm thrown upon some of the inmates I work with. Most of the time, these prisoners are in hand cuffs and immobile and yet officers will treat them as animals and have no respect for their humanity. I've seen a man in handcuffs and leg cuffs in the fetal position, on the ground, getting kicked by officers. To me, those cops are weak. They're cowards, both mentally and morally. If for some reason I find it necessary to use force or hit an accused or convicted criminal, I make certain they have no restraints so it would be a fair fight. They have no chance of winning, regardless, but I'll at least make the playing field even.

But, again, if the accused or convicted treat me right, I'll treat them right. They have my sympathy and empathy.

The 'criminals' who I have the most compassion for are those who I believe don't even belong in jail in the first place. Take, for example, a person charged with possession of illegal substances with intent to distribute. I have met inmates who are serving 5 or 10 year sentences because they were caught with a small sack of marijuana. Something like that is uncalled for and frankly, I think it's silly. So what if a person is caught with marijuana or ecstasy or any other light drug. People who do drugs like that are common and it's a shame some cops uphold this ridiculous law. If police arrested everyone who did any type of illegal drug, half the population would be in jail. The system can be totally wrong in some cases . . .

I believe a bit of morality, common sense and understanding needs to be implemented by cops while on duty. Sometimes the uniform and job description shouldn't be taken so literally. A police officer needs to look deep within one's self to determine the proper thing to do every day. They are held up on a sort of pedestal compared to civilians and they need to earn that status by using these feelings and instincts correctly.

My life has taught me so much already and it's time for me to use this knowledge for good. It will make me one of the best in the field and will make my work much easier and more efficient than others. Most other officers have lived a big majority of their lives in a bubble, unexposed to the realities of society. Their eyes see only a pin point on a vast canvas. My eyes capture the entire picture, fusing with every brush stroke.